Old Ebbw Vale

in photographs

Vol. 2

1 (*Overleaf*) Casting 'C' Furnace, Ebbw Vale Works, *c.*1958

Old Ebbw Vale

in photographs

VOLUME 2

by

Keith Thomas

FOREWORD
by

J. H. Powell, M.C.

STEWART WILLIAMS, PUBLISHERS

BARRY

First published in October, 1980

© Stewart Williams, Publishers,
Bryn Awel, Buttrills Road,
Barry, South Glamorgan

ISBN 0 900807 41 5

To my Father and Mother

Printed in Wales by D. Brown & Sons Ltd., Cowbridge and Bridgend, Glamorgan

Foreword

by J. H. POWELL, M.C.,

Director of The British Steel Corporation
Associated Products Group and Vice-Chairman of
The Sports Council for Wales

I was delighted to learn that Keith Thomas had decided to produce a second volume of his successful pictorial history of Ebbw Vale. It is a great honour to have been asked to contribute a few words as a foreword.

I was associated with the Steelworks between 1957 and 1970 and rate these years as the happiest and most rewarding of my life.

As the General Manager of the biggest employer in the area one was expected not only to manage the Steelworks but quite rightly to take an active interest in the varied life of the community. My association with the old Ebbw Vale Urban District Council was one I particularly cherish because it enabled me to rub shoulders with some of the most astute and forward thinking people I have ever met. I was particularly interested in the welfare of the Senior Citizens, spurred on by Miss Maisie Herbert to do great and at times seemingly impossible deeds on their behalf.

Sport in the area was always considered important and to me it was a great joy to participate in a whole range of activities with so many of the people one worked alongside in the Steelworks. It was a point of honour to completely forget and never mention any differences which might occur in work and this unbroken rule applied to every aspect of community life.

Looking through the earliest photographs of the town and the community I was much better able to understand the character of the people, many of whose descendants I had the privilege to work with and I commend Keith's effort in this second volume to remind us of things past that should never be forgotten.

For me Ebbw Vale was a labour of love and represented what I value most in Wales, a truly classless society.

Introduction

Many families in Ebbw Vale have roots which go back into the past for over two hundred years and it is therefore with great pride that members of these families have seen the town and its industries grow and develop, despite periods of hardship which have struck deeply into the town's prosperity. Their pride in the community now gives rise to a sense of frustration in seeing the source of their work and therefore their financial stability disappearing. I feel it is important at this time to review our history in order to reassure ourselves that the town has a past to be proud of, and a future for which we must fight, as our predecessors did, even though the odds are great.

The 1980s may prove to be the most dramatic years in the history of Ebbw Vale. Changes have marked the town's history, the first being the introduction of iron-making at Beaufort in 1780, and at Ebbw Vale in 1790. The year 1844 saw the coming of the wealthier iron-masters and in 1860 a major advance in metal manufacture by the introduction of steel-making. The year 1899 brought technology into the works with the appointment of Frederick Mills as the first technically trained managing director who reshaped and rebuilt the works.

After the lean years of the nineteen twenties, 1938 saw the beginning of a new concept in the making and treatment of steel. A period of enormous effort was rewarded by great prosperity which transformed the town. The 1960s brought big changes in transport and communications with the decline of steam and rail, and great improvement to roads by the opening of the Heads of the Valleys Road, which gave easier access to Swansea and the Midlands. The 80s will see changes in the employment pattern. A few basic industries will be to some extent replaced by many smaller firms; trade will alter as a result of superstores and a new pattern of commerce will emerge. The population of the area, which climbed to over 40,000 in 1919 and has now dropped to 24,000, will probably continue to diminish unless there is an investment by some large international industrialist employing over 3,000 people. This would then attract subsidiary industries. The areas occupied by the old works will be re-developed and this could, once again, bring prosperity. But whatever the future may be, one thing is certain: great changes will take place and become in themselves part of the history of the town, and of interest to young readers in future families.

Looking through the photographs we can see in the town views the way in which people have invested in building and rebuilding their own property. Some were ambitious and others were very humble. It is interesting to compare the different styles of development and changes in the way of life. Sport and entertainment have helped to relieve the pressures. Great friendships and happy memories have been cherished from an association with rugby and soccer teams and group activities of all kinds. It is impossible to cover all sports and pastimes, or to add the names of all the people in each photograph, but it is pleasurable to try to remember half-forgotten faces. Perhaps we have not made as much progress with our roads and public transport as we would have wished, but we have progressed a long way from the stage coach! The life of the churches has been sadly neglected during recent years. Somehow a part of our community life has disappeared, but this is not for the first time, and perhaps a revival of a different kind is just around the corner. The photographs tell of a time when 'Sunday Best' clothes were a necessity for respectability, when great fun was had and valued friendships were made, and a time when the spiritual side of life was important in daily living. Religion has been linked with Education because of its importance in the life of the children of the town. And what memories there are of the teachers! Schooldays leave us with mixed feelings but the standard of Education in Ebbw Vale must surely have been hard to equal.

There has never been a shortage of people to take an active part in the service of the town and the section dealing with this carries us over a period of more than a hundred years in war and peace. The housing of the town was provided by the 'captains of industry' and by private investment, and without the benefit of Local Government planning. Since 1900 private investment has decreased and the principal additions and improvements to housing have been left mainly as the responsibility of the Urban and Borough Councils, but the introduction of improvement grants has helped Ebbw Valians to improve older properties.

While there were many people who were delighted with the 'Caswell' photograph in Volume 1, because they were related to this large family, hundreds of others were able to find family links in many other photographs. Both books will become in future everybody's family album.

I hope that this book will bring lasting pleasure to all who scan its pages. 'One picture is worth a thousand words' so it is said, and after publishing volume one of *Old Ebbw Vale in Photographs* I have to agree with this sentiment as each photograph has more than one story to tell. Apart from my own collection, so many people have offered photographs and shown such interest that I was persuaded to publish this second volume, and I am aware that many more fascinating photographs exist, many of which I have had to leave out to keep a balance in the selection and satisfy the requirements of my publisher. Once again I would like to express my gratitude to those who, over the years, have taken photographs, like Mr Chilcott of Beaufort, Mr Davies of Victoria Road, and Mr Lloyd of Cwm and the many amateur photographers as well as those who have made collections of photographs. I would also wish to thank those who have offered help and those who have given me such encouragement in the production of both books, particularly my wife.

Keith Thomas

The Town and Surroundings

2 Palace Theatre and Cinema built as the Central Hall in 1892 and originally seating 1,500. Later alterations gave it the largest stage in South Wales, with a proscenium measuring forty-three feet wide and stage forty-five feet deep. It then seated 900

3 Old Rassau viewed from the viaduct, *c.*1925

4 Lower Rassau, *c.*1924, showing Powell's Row, which is now the site of the Tai Bach Aged
Persons Bungalows

5/6 After severe snowstorms in the winter of 1947 the town was cut off by road and rail for over a week. No buses ran for seven weeks, not even 'Offies'!

TREVIL, NR. BEAUFORT

7 Not exactly 'Trefil', but the site of the Trefil Machine, which weighed limestone from the quarries, and the L.N.W.R. Trefil Halt is in the cutting

8 Beaufort Rise, *c.*1920

9 'Six Roads', 1950. Mr Percy Miles, 'Glynfab' of the *Merthyr Express*, walks home (*left*) from night duty as a Richard Thomas and Baldwin telephonist. Between them Mr Miles and his father gave press coverage for over 80 years

10 James Street, 1960

11 The Big Arch was built in 1813. The river arch was first built in 1790, and the old road arch in 1861. The pedestrian arch was constructed in 1964

12 Market Street, c.1930. On the right hand side is the Market Hall which was built in 1885 and housed the Urban District Council Offices. Outside is advertised the film of the Wembley Cup Final

The County Corner, (5 Roads) Ebbw Vale. 287

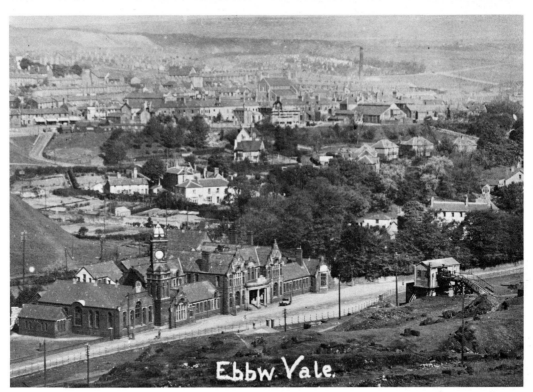

13 A view of the town centre in 1938

14 The Drill Ground and Gorsedd Park in 1961

15 Bethcar Terrace, *c.*1907

16 Armoury Terrace, *c.*1910
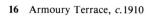

17 Bethcar Street, *c.*1920

18 'Pond Buildings', 1937, still add distinction to the town

19 Armoury Terrace, *c.*1910. Armoury shop was owned by Alfred Jones who invested his capital in developing the town

20 Church Street, *c.*1906. A bustling centre of commerce

21 Victoria Road, *c.*1900. The timber stock of the undertakers lines the footpath on the left

22 Ebbw Vale, 1900. A north-westerly wind keeps Newtown free of dust for the day

Ebbw Vale. General View.

23 Augusta Street, c.1911

24 Park Place, Waunlwyd, c.1947. Postmaster Mr Morgan and his wife wait for customers

25/26 Two views of Cwm *c.*1904 and *c.*1908 from Mr Lloyd's extensive collection of plate photographs of the town's development. Each square inch has some interesting feature

27   Station Terrace, Cwm, a busy shopping centre, *c*.1910

28   Troed y rhiw y Myrdd Fach. This farm was behind Tirzah Chapel, Cwm

Sports and Entertainments

29   Ebbw Vale Rugby Football Club. Captain 'Dai' Reagan Jones (*seated centre*)

30 First Professional Rugby team, Chairman T. J. Rees, 1907

31 Vicar Llewellyn (*left*) was a keen supporter of every aspect of community life

32 A team ready to take on all challengers—Ebbw Vale A.F.C., 1913-1914

33 This team must have been successful with Louis Berni on the committee!

34 Victoria United Soccer team, winners of Mill's Cup, 1923

35 Newtown Rovers, 1922. In the group are Con McCarthy, Cy Winstone, Tommy (Sapper) Ghee, captain, Joe Morgan, goalkeeper Harold Boulter and the little girl was Peggy Gardner

36 Waunlwyd Albions. This type of team encouraged soccer stars like Ron Burgess and Doug Witcomb of Cwm Villa Boys' Club

37 Cwm Betterment Club, 1931. The goalkeeper was Stan Burgess and the captain Charlie Ricketts

38 Ebbw Vale All Saints School football team, 1924. The captain was Amos Williams

39 Welsh Schools' Football International, Wales v Scotland at Cardiff, 1925. Ebbw Vale was represented by Amos Williams and Association Chairman, E. H. Jones, who was later to become the first headmaster of Glyncoed Senior School

40   Cwm Junior School, 1958, photographed by Keith Davies. The captain of the team was David
Lewis and the goalkeeper, Brian Clegg

41   A keen group of Ebbw Vale Gymnasts, *c.*1914

42 A busy scene at the lido, *c.*1935

43 Waunlwyd and Victoria Cycling Club, 1902

44 Beaufort Bowling Club, 1950, with President Dr Stein and the Stein Cup

45 Marine Colliery Cricket Team, 1953. The captain was Tom Jones

46 A Whit-Monday crowd at Victoria Park, the local beauty spot which was created by Thomas Brown, the works' manager in 1850

47 'Anyone for tennis?' Victoria and Waunlwyd Welfare Ground

Tennis Courts & Pavilion. Victoria & Waunllwyd Welfare Grounds

48 David Davies (*right*) enjoying a ride on the mountain at Hilltop

49 Miss Tamblin, daughter of the licensee of the *Rhyd y Blew*, with her horse, groomed to perfection for a show

50 This fire engine was borrowed from Newport for the Coronation carnival in 1937.

51 First prize in the Beaufort Carnival, *c.*1920, went to 'Two Country Women', Mrs P. Roberts and Miss Wilding

52 Miss Rachel James stands proudly with her class on Saint David's Day, in the early 20s

53 Waunlwyd 'Nibs' carnival group in the early 20s

54 Firemen in their brass helmets escort carnival queen Clarice Wallace (now Mrs Treharn)

55 The 'Old Village Choir' from Carmel pause for a photograph near Greenfield Crescent on the way to a Carnival in 1937

56 The Rajah (Des Williams) with his slaves and slave master Cliff England, *c*.1958

57 Residents of Rhyd y Cae at the 1953 Coronation tea party. County Councillor Harry Phillips
is on the left

59   Residents of Emlyn Avenue enjoying a day out at Weston, *c*.1947

60   The Ebbw Vale fire engine stands in the Council yard ready for the carnival, *c*.1930. The group was called 'Ladies of the League of Nations'

62 Royal Breconian Glee Men, 1916. Conductor, Spencer Hill. Members of this group and the one below were prominent in musical and public events for over fifty years

63 The Black and White Minstrels, *c.*1935, with their conductor, Charlie Jones

Transport

64 This stage coach and its contemporaries were the principal means of travel, apart from the
railways, up to 1917

65 This photograph superimposed on an old advertisement shows a charabanc outing for Colliery officials in 1919

66 A charabanc outing for Caersalem Chapel, *c.*1922

67 Low bridges in the valleys posed a problem for 'double deckers', but this one at Cemetery Road clears 13 feet 4½ inches

68 Beaufort Station, 1947, when weather conditions made travelling impossible

69 Ebbw Vale L.M.S. Station, *c.*1925

70 A train passes under the 'Big Arch' at the Great
Western Station in 1920

71 The last pannier tank 0-6-0 engine to leave Ebbw Vale Station (goods only)

72 This engine is part of a much larger portrait of Thomas Brown painted in 1854. It was made by Neilsons of Glasgow and was one of a fleet of locos used at Ebbw Vale and at the Brendon Hill mines

73 The 'Ebbw Vale', one of the specially designed 'Peckett' locos purchased in 1904 when the Ebbw Vale Company renewed its stock

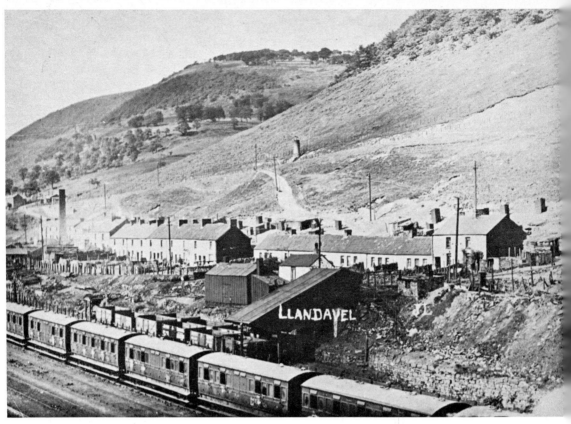

74 Llandavel village, a busy community which existed long before Cwm was built

75 Tredegar Road Bridge and the L.M.S. Station, prior to demolition

Religion and Education

76   Another of Mr Lloyd's photographic gems! The corrugated chapel was later removed from
Cwm to become the 'Tin Tab' at the Grammar School, Ebbw Vale

77 Interior of Caersalem chapel, *c.*1890, showing the oil lamps and the deacon's 'sêt fawr'

78 With the demolition of 'Old Caersalem' in 1938 a temporary home was found at Victoria Institute. This photograph shows the last Whit-walk from the Institute in 1952

79 Caersalem Baptist Chapel, built by the workers from the Victoria Ironworks (founded 1837). The determination of these men resulted in the building of the new chapel in 1930, shown below

80 Tea in the new Caersalem, 1952

The Church, Ebbw Vale

81 Christ Church, declared the 'Cathedral of the Hills', at its opening on 8 December, 1861, by the Rev. A. Olivant, Lord Bishop of Llandaff. It was built under the patronage of Abraham Darby, IV

82 The Church choir, *c.*1914

83 Rev. John Evans, B.A., Vicar of Christ Church
1910-1921. During his ministry, Sir Frederick Mills
donated, in 1919, the four-faced clock

84 The induction of Rev. Oliver Davies, B.A., R.D., Vicar from 1934-1964

85 Visit of Bishop Green (*centre*) with Vicar Alfred Griffiths of Christ Church, 1921-33 (*left*), and (*right*) Vicar of New Quay Rev. Evans, *c.*1930

86 Rev. Davies, one of the faithful curates of Christ Church

87 St. Mary's Church, Victoria, *c.*1920

88 St. John's Church, Ebbw Vale, *c.*1925 during the ministry of Vicar Hill (1922-31) who tragically died in a motor car accident

89 Rev. Dr Thomas Rees, D.D., Minister of Carmel Independent Chapel, Beaufort, from 1849-1862. He survived cholera caught while sick visiting, and became the author of a classic work *The History of Protestant Nonconformity in Wales*, published in 1861

90 Members of Carmel, Whit-Monday, 1934. (*Centre*) the Minister, Rev. Clifford Bevan

91 A Model 'T' Ford has the audacity to pass a procession in 1922!

92 Park Road Victoria Methodists, with Rev. W. Taggart, *c.*1906

93 A dry and sunny Whit-Monday with pretty hats and dresses and the men in straw 'bengies',
*c.*1920

94 A Corpus Christi procession for the children of All Saint's Catholic Church, 1926. On the far
right is Pat Sheen (Mrs A. Williams), and in front is Connie Chapman

95 Leaders of James Street Methodist Chapel, 1953, with the Minister, Rev. A. Altree

96 A practice for the Whit-Monday chorus, *c.*1960. The minister was Rev. G. H. Daniels

97 The Minister, Rev. E. Jeremiah, and the deacons of Libanus Congregational Chapel, September, 1959

98 Whit-Monday, 1952, outside the 'Gin Shop'. The Minister was the Rev. A. Altree and at his side is the circuit steward, John Gibbs

99 A group of Ebbw Vale Salvation Army workers, 1928, with Captain Good. General Booth preached in Penuel Chapel in July, 1879

100 Sunday School Concert, 1934, at Saron Chapel

101   Rassau School, built in 1878. It was typical of the 'Local Board' schools built in the area.
Photograph taken in 1935

102   Rassau School, Class 1b, 1925. Teacher, Miss Jenkins (Mrs Tom Jones)

103 Standard III, Rassau School, 1897. Teacher, Mrs Jenkins

104 Standard II at Beaufort Hill School, *c.*1922. The teacher was Miss Jenkins

105 Headmaster Mr John Lewis and teacher Mr Cooper, with a smart class in 1911 at Briery Hill School. Mr Lewis, 'The Mount', was headmaster of the Forge School and Briery Hill for 49 years. He was also choirmaster at Christ Church for fifty-one years. He died in 1924, aged 80

106 Miss Harris with her class at Waunlwyd School, *c.*1926

107 A class at Cwm Infants, 1913. The teacher was Florrie Self

108 Waunlwyd School, 1911. Headmaster, Mr Griffiths, teacher, Mr Evans

109   Mr J. R. Morgan, well respected Head of the Grammar School, with the staff

The photographs on these two pages are taken from the 1912 Ebbw Vale
Grammar School Brochure

110   Mr 'Josh' Jones' form

111   Mr T. L. Williams' form

112   Mr D. R. Roberts' form

113 Grammar school hockey team, 1945. Headmaster D. T. Davies, Headmistress Miss H. M. Williams and Gym Mistress Miss Lindberg

114 Grammar School prefects, 1945

Industry and Trade

115   Aerial view of Ebbw Vale works, c.1950. The most modern in Europe in 1938

The Ebbw Vale Steel, Iron & Coal Company Ld. Ebbw Vale. Mon.

Head Office: Ebbw Vale.
London Office: 122. Cannon St.
Birmingham. Glasgow.
Cardiff & Newport.

Colliery. Proprietors
Makers of
PIG IRON
Spiegleisen & Ferro-Manganese
STEEL RAILS,
TIN BARS,
&c. &c.

Telegraphic Addresses:
FURNACES: LONDON.
COMPANY: EBBW-VALE.

General View of Ebbw-Vale. (Eastern Portion)

(*opposite*) The Ebbw Vale furnaces, seen here in 1900, began in 1790. The Ebbw Vale House is in the foreground

117   General view of Ebbw Vale works, *c.*1900

118   Furnace Brickworks 1900, now the Cwm Draw Industrial site

The Ebbw-Vale Steel, Iron & Coal Co.Ld.

COLLIERIES.

No. 6 Pit, Victoria.

Red Ash Colliery.

No. 5 Pit, Victoria.

No. 22 Pit, Ebbw Vale.

Engine Pit, Sirhowy.

No. 9 Pit, Sirhowy.

120 The last winding engineman at the Prince of Wales Pit, Victoria, Mr Len Brain, at his seat in the 'pulpit'. Two days later the motors burned out and the pit closed one week prematurely on 30 January, 1974. The pit, 188 yards in depth, was the first to have electrical winding engines

121 No. 5, Prince of Wales Pit. The tip adjacent was removed to create the Hilltop Sports Ground and a site for new fitting shops in 1953. (Compare old No. 5 in photograph **119**)

122 The 'heavy end' of the Ebbw Vale works in 1955

123 Tyn y fyd farm mill and the pump house. The wooded hillside became the site for Waunlwyd

124 A group of Ebbw Vale Company office workers at the seaside in Aberystwyth, *c.*1900

125 Officials and workers of the Ebbw Vale Company, *c.*1910

(*opposite*) Ready to cast 'C' furnace. Workers faced danger every day on the iron making plant

127 Departmental managers of Ebbw Vale Company enjoying an evening out, *c*.1934

128 Mr Fowler (*centre*) with the blast furnace staff, 1946

129/130 David Davies the Grocer was an enterprising man in his early days at Ebbw Vale in 1890. This was his first shop, *c.*1905. His sons expanded the business and the photograph below shows how the shop looked in 1935

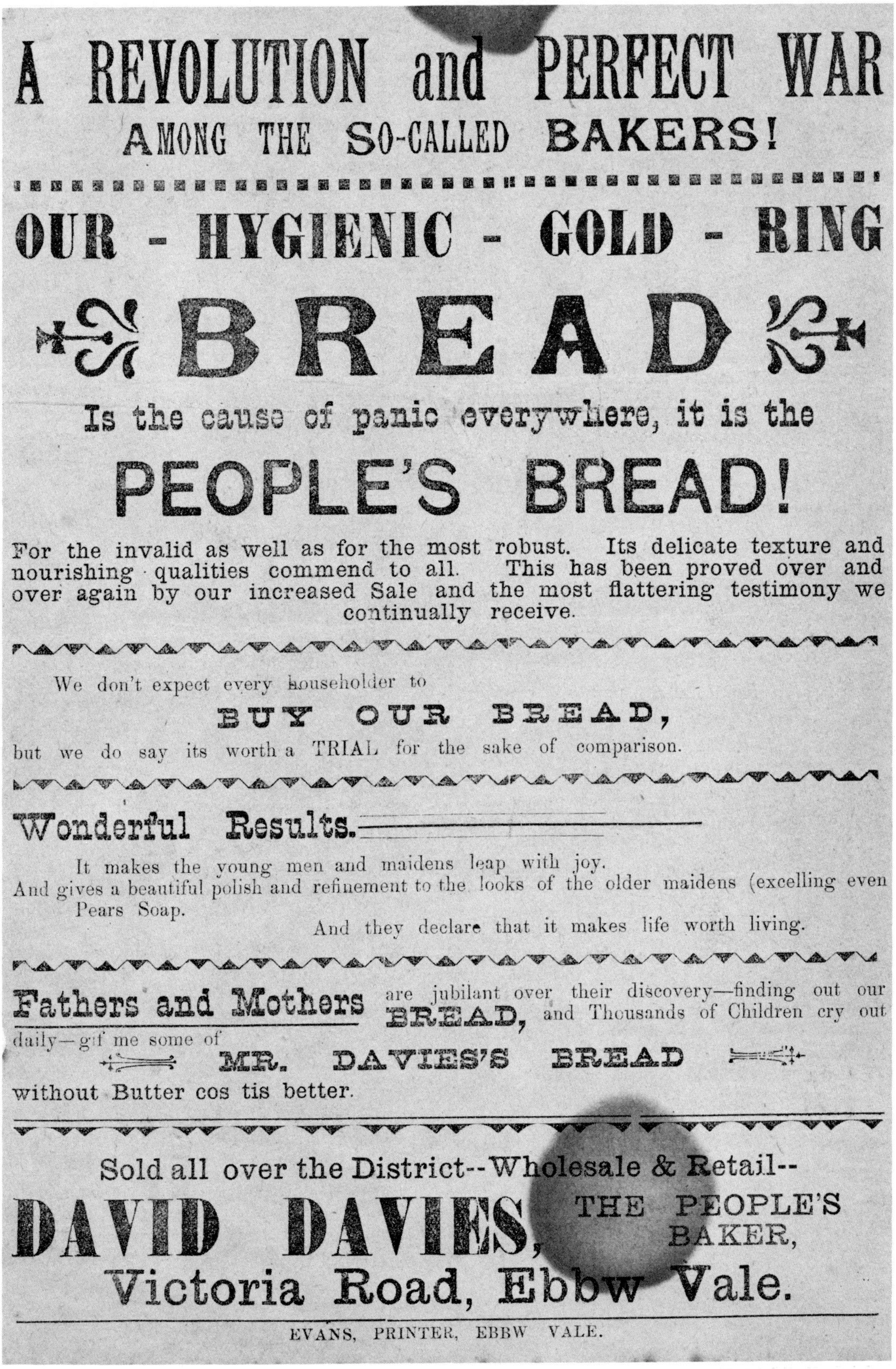

131 Who could resist such a convincing advertisement!

132 Front room shops were a feature of valley life. This shop in William Street was owned by Henry Grubb, *c*.1920

133 A busy grocer's shop in Spencer Street, next to Saron Chapel, 1927

134 General dealer, Ben Grubb, stands in the doorway of his shop, which has now become Phillipe's, the hair stylists

135 This shop is still a newsagent's today—Garrods. In the doorway is Miss Ada Davies (Mrs Beynon), *c*.1915

136 Ebbw Vale Post Office in Church Street, 1900

137 Post Office staff, *c*.1920, taken at the rear of the County Building's Post Office

138 An obviously prosperous milkman and his staff in Augusta Street, Victoria, *c.*1930

139 Harrison & Sons, the ironmongers, Market Street, *c.*1900, and still going stong. James Harrison, the founder, came to the area in 1864 and started the business in 1874 at Pontygof

Public Service and Special Events

140 The first Royal visit to Ebbw Vale, 21 February, 1918, when Prince Edward was greeted at the General Offices by the Chairman of the Council, Charles Morgan. The Prince was accompanied by his private secretary, Sir Sydney Greville, and also Col. W. Charles Wright

141 Brecknockshire Volunteer Band of Beaufort, *c*.1865, under the leadership of Mr Sage

142 The locally enlisted 3rd Mons. (Mill's Army) go to war, 1914, from Ebbw Vale Station

143 The Second-World-War 3rd Mons. at Rostrevor in 1941. The officer-in-charge was Col. George Cooper.

144 Third Mons. band at Rostrevor, 1941. On 'D' Day they went to France as stretcher bearers and were captured. The Bandmaster was W. Rodgers

145 Cwm Brigade of St John's Ambulance Corps, 1927. They were first on the scene at the Marine Colliery disaster. Dr Florance O'Sullivan is in the centre of the front row

146 Ebbw Vale Battalion of the Home Guard, c.1943

147 Some members of the Home Guard at camp in Manmoel, 1943

148 Church Parade, 1946, and the Red Cross march smartly up Armoury Hill

149 Tom Morgan, M.C., Ebbw Vale's first O.B.E., at Buckingham Palace. His wife is on his right hand; niece, Bette Davies (Mrs Amos), is on his left. The award was given to him in 1945 for services to the L.D.V. and Home Guard

150 The first M.B.E. in Ebbw Vale, Councillor Tom Thomas with his wife at St James' Palace in 1938. He received the award for long service to the community and for his Chairmanship of the Local Employment Exchange Committee during the depression

151   Civic dignitaries at the opening of Glyncoed Junior School, 1939. Chairman of the Council
was Mrs E. M. Honeyfield

152   The Needs and Comforts Fund committee, 1939-1945, which organised concerts and sent
gifts to the local soldiers in P.O.W. camps and on active service. The Chairman was Edgar Harries

153 Council staff enjoying an annual outing, 1935

154 The opening ceremony at the new Filtration Plant at Carno Reservoir, 1951. Councillor Tal. Nicholas (*centre*) and J. Grafton Hoskins (*left, centre*), Engineer and Surveyor to the Council

155   Cwm detachment of the Fire Brigade, 1910. Lazarus Coombes, who served for over twenty years from May 1898, was made Officer-in-Charge in 1906

156   Cwm Fire Brigade with their first motor vehicle, 1914

157 Ebbw Vale Fire Brigade, c.1935

158 P.C. Ron Lewis in 1910. At seventeen he was the youngest constable in Monmouthshire

159 Ebbw Vale Police Station, 1911. The scene of the Jewish Riots, August 1911. Inspector J. Price stands outside. He spent forty years in the Monmouthshire Constabulary, joining in 1871

160 The scouts celebrate seventy years of youth activity in 1980. These photographs show the 50th Anniversary Parade in July 1960

161 Elwyn Thomas (*left*) being presented with the Order of Merit by Major General T. W. Rees. Mr Thomas also received the Silver Wolf Award in recognition of over 50 years' service to the Scout Movement

162 Some of the guests at a Civic reception held at Beaufort Ballroom after the Welsh Youth Rugby Match in March 1957

163 Mr and Mrs Caron put the final touches to the floral arrangements for the civic reception for the Duke of Edinburgh's visit, July 1958

164 T. J. Thomas, the surveyor from 1883 to 1922, inspects the site of Carno Reservoir with Mr Gourley the consultant and Mr Hardwick the caretaker, c.1905

165 The Council scavenging cart, about 1915

166 Looking forward to their day trip, holiday makers on Beaufort Station, *c.*1925

167 Councillor John Holman, chairman, and his daughter Doris, accompany a celebrity in a
Rolls Royce, 1916

168 Matron Gould and staff of the Isolation Hospital, now the site of Plas y Coed, in 1905. Back row (*left to right*) Councillor Thomas Morgan (Coed y Gric), Curate Phillips, Vicar Llewellyn and Mr Hughes, the solicitor

169 Confirmation class at St Paul's Church, Cwm, c.1945. The Vicar is Rev. Basil Williams

170 Some eager spectators in Badminton Grove on the day of the Duke of Edinburgh's visit

Housing

171 Commercial Street, Briery Hill, *c.*1949. An example of early development which up to 1854 had no sanitation or refuse collection

172 Queen Street, Victoria, named after the Queen, was built in 1837

173 Rees Street, built in 1850, now demolished to make way for new development

174 The two communities of Church Town and Chapel Town were joined by Bethcar Street, c.1905. The photograph shows the Drill Ground pond and the railway line to Eureka Place, before development

175 High Street, Briery Hill, 1949

176 Lethbridge Terrace, built 1837-1839 and named after Sir Thomas Lethbridge, senior partner in the Monmouthshire Iron Company, who first developed the Victoria Iron works

177 Changes in the river level caused flooding at Marine Street, December, 1960

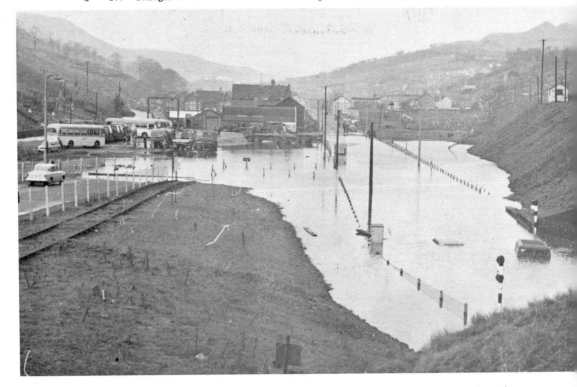

178 Inspector J. Price and his wife stand outside their new home in 1911. Members of their family still serve the community at Badminton Grove Post Office

179 A back view of Badminton Grove showing a duck pond near the *Beaufort Arms*

180 Badminton Grove, 1911, with sheep dog trials on Mortimer's Field, and the Co-op and Tranters being built

181 Rhyd-y-cae housing site, *c.*1933

Personalities

182 Field Marshal Montgomery being introduced to Tom Thomas, M.B.E., by Chairman, Councillor Jack Bush, on 23 September, 1948

183   The Field Marshal at Marine Colliery Pit Head Baths, with Vice-Chairman Councillor
Bert Thomas

184   The cavalcade passes Victoria School and headmaster Alonzo Boore, while the loco driver
whistles a salute

185 Stephen D. Morris, J.P., and his wife, c.1933.
A leading tradesman in the town and son of William
Morris, whose photograph appeared in Volume 1

186 Mr D. Jones, one of Ebbw Vale's
most loved and respected musicians,
who conducted the Ebbw Vale Choral
Society for 43 years. The choir began in
the 1860s and finished in July 1979

187 At the Welfare Ground, April 1959, Mr Eugene Cross (now Sir Eugene) listens attentively to 'Nye', at the unveiling of the Sir William Firth Gates. The Welfare ground is now called the Eugene Cross Park, in honour of Sir Eugene's personal efforts over more than fifty years to improve the welfare facilities in the town

188 The First World War claimed the lives of many courageous Ebbw Vale men. For outstanding heroism local man Jack Williams was awarded the Victoria Cross, D.C.M., M.M. and Bar and Médaille Militaire

189 The Memorial Plaque at Christ Church

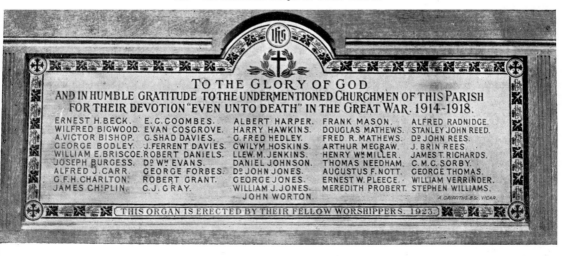

TO THE GLORY OF GOD

AND IN HUMBLE GRATITUDE TO THE UNDERMENTIONED CHURCHMEN OF THIS PARISH FOR THEIR DEVOTION "EVEN UNTO DEATH" IN THE GREAT WAR. 1914-1918.

ERNEST H. BECK.	E. C. COOMBES.	ALBERT HARPER.	FRANK MASON.	ALFRED RADNIDGE.
WILFRED BIGWOOD.	EVAN COSGROVE.	HARRY HAWKINS.	DOUGLAS MATHEWS.	STANLEY JOHN REED.
A. VICTOR BISHOP.	G. SHAD DAVIES.	G. FRED HEDLEY.	FRED R. MATHEWS.	Dʳ JOHN REES.
GEORGE BODLEY.	J. FERRENT DAVIES.	GWILYM HOSKINS.	ARTHUR MEGRAW.	J. BRIN REES.
WILLIAM E. BRISCOE.	ROBERT DANIELS.	LLEW. M. JENKINS.	HENRY Wᵐ MILLER.	JAMES T. RICHARDS.
JOSEPH BURGESS.	Dʳ Wᵐ EVANS.	DANIEL JOHNSON.	THOMAS NEEDHAM.	C. M. C. SORBY.
ALFRED J. CARR.	GEORGE FORBES.	Dʳ JOHN JONES.	AUGUSTUS F. NOTT.	GEORGE THOMAS.
G. F. H. CHARLTON.	ROBERT GRANT.	GEORGE JONES.	ERNEST W. PLEECE.	WILLIAM VERRINDER.
JAMES CHIPLIN.	C. J. GRAY.	WILLIAM J. JONES.	MEREDITH PROBERT.	STEPHEN WILLIAMS.
		JOHN WORTON.		

A. GRIFFITHS. B.Sc. VICAR.

THIS ORGAN IS ERECTED BY THEIR FELLOW WORSHIPPERS. 1923.

191 Well-known traders in Ebbw Vale, the Carini Brothers, Beaufort Rise, *c.*1921

192 Briery Hill's smallest pub, with the licensee, Bill Morgan, on the right

193 Ron Burgess, Captain of Tottenham Hotspur and Wales, was born in Cwm. A brilliant left half, he also represented Wales in the 1948 Great Britain side and became the first Welshman to play for the Football League XI

194 Burgess 'holding-off' the immortal Stanley Matthews at White Hart Lane *c.*1950

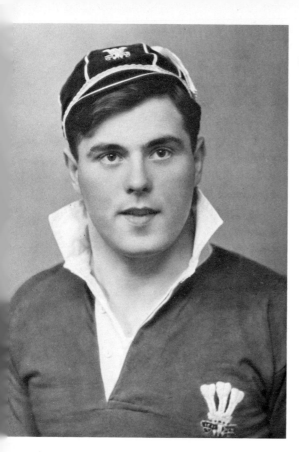

195 Graham Powell, Ebbw Vale's first international rugby player. For a time, head of Physics at Hafod y Ddol County School, and now a managing director of Total Oil

196 Bill Sullivan, one of the many local sportsmen who became professionals

197 'Paddy' Sheen and the Duffryn School choir, 1953, with accompanist Mrs May Parry. Both have made a large contribution to the fine musical reputation of the town

198 Ben Davies, now 93, on the day of his release from the army in 1919, with two pals from Waunlwyd, on a Harley Davison

199 Variety and television star, Victor Spinetti, a dashing young man *c.*1950

200 Emlyn Williams and Edwin Thomas, leaders of a men's dancing class in Cwm, which was held in premises over a bakery in School Terrace, *c.*1925

Acknowledgements

I would like to express my grateful thanks to the following individuals and organisations for allowing me to use their photographs:

Civic Collection (1, 58, 115, 126, 154, 162, 163, 170, 171, 172, 175, 187); Graham Jones (3, 4, 6, 34, 44, 45, 51, 52, 55, 57, 90, 91, 101, 102, 103, 104, 167); Radnor Rees (5, 6); Keith Davies (8, 24, 25, 26, 28, 36, 40, 42, 43, 46, 47, 53, 66, 70, 74, 76, 77, 78, 79, 80, 107, 108, 123, 136, 137, 138, 165, 174, 184); Mr Wakely (29); Glenys Lewis (32, 56, 58, 61, 132, 134, 148, 158); S. Burgess (33, 37); C. Winstone (35); Mrs P. Williams (38, 39, 94, 179); C. Healy (49, 62); Mrs Howells (54, 99); G. Beynon (63, 135); T. Rowson (73); Mrs E. Marchant (92, 124); D. E. Jones (97); Miss Briscoe (100, 133, 152); Mr Morris (109, 110, 111, 112); Mr Wilcox (116, 118, 119); Mr Langford (117); J. E. Watkins (125, 127); J. J. Thomas (128, 150); E. Harrison (139); Mrs Morgan (140, 149, 185); H. Wall (141, 166); Mrs Duggan (142); G. H. Brown (143, 144, 145); Miss M. Herbert (153); F. Coombes (27, 155, 156, 183); Anne Jones (157); J. Price (159, 178); W. Thomas (160, 161); Mrs Gray (164); Mrs D. Hopkins (168); Mr Morgan (188); B. Sidoli (190); Mr Carini (191); Mrs Bayliss (194); Mrs E. Powell (195); Mrs Jukes (196); Mrs M. Chard (197); B. Davies (198); Mrs Spinetti (199); Mrs Phelps (146); Mrs Annett (106)

CORRECTIONS TO VOLUME 1

Photographs   **46** The mascot was Terry Flanagan
75 The date was 1925
109 A view of No. 1 Pit
117 Men of the Bessemer Department
120 The date was c.1901
143 Sister Rose and her husband
146 (*Right*) view of Gantre Row
147 (*Below*) Sychfos Row and Willowtown about 1895
160 Delete (*centre*)
184 Mr and Mrs William Morris
193 The date is nearer 1921

LITTLE FALLS CARRY. Before a canal was built at the little falls in the Mohawk River, boats known as bateaux had to be portaged around the falls and rapids using improvised carriages and oxen, as shown in this drawing. Land on the south side of the river was granted to Hendrick and Johan Jost Herkimer, and records show that early on, they engaged in this enterprise. (Courtesy of *Heroes and Legends of the Mohawk Valley* print series, Alan Sterling, historian, and Gary Zaboly, artists.)

ON THE COVER: *Life* magazine photojournalist Alfred Eisenstaedt came to Little Falls on July 25, 1945, to take this group photograph in Eastern Park for his unpublished photographic essay "A Town at War." (Courtesy of the authors.)

IMAGES
of America

LITTLE FALLS

Susan R. Perkins
and Caryl A. Hopson

ARCADIA
PUBLISHING

Published by Arcadia Publishing
Charleston, South Carolina

Library of Congress Control Number: 2010928793

For all general information, please contact Arcadia Publishing:
Telephone 843-853-2070
Fax 843-853-0044
E-mail sales@arcadiapublishing.com
For customer service and orders:
Toll-Free 1-888-313-2665

Visit us on the Internet at www.arcadiapublishing.com

This book is dedicated to all of the residents
of Little Falls, past and present.

CONTENTS

ACKNOWLEDGMENTS

A big thank you to the following people for making this book possible: to our friends at Little Falls Historical Society (LFHS), for sharing their valuable collection of photographs with us and to their wonderful volunteers, who were always available to assist us, including Heather Dawes, our "go-to" girl, who went above and beyond finding information for us and knowing the right person to talk to; Louie Baum, for sharing his knowledge of Little Falls and fact-checking our captions; Louie Baum and Jeff Gressler for writing our introduction; and Mary Alice Rieman and David Dinneen for identifying people. We'd like to thank our volunteers at the Herkimer County Historical Society: Steve Knight, for helping write captions in the midst of genealogy requests; Alta DeLong, for caption-writing between census work; Jeff Steele, for lending a hand with captions; Mary Haefele, Dolores Lyman, Ann Pierce, and Linda Pratt for helping research; and our student intern Mary Cirillo, who is always up to the task, whatever we ask of her. This book wouldn't be possible without the people who have donated pictures: Owen and Sharon Brown (Beavers, Wetlands, and Wildlife), Clete McLaughlin (Benton Hall Academy), Ann Blask, Esther Brown, Margaret Goldman (Burrows Paper Corporation), Camp Russell, Patricia Carey, Nancy Cioch, Kendall Cole, Janet Crimmins, Fr. Rafal Dadello, Barry Dawson, Andria DeLisle-Heath (Red Cross), David Dinneen, Kyle Brown (Feldmeier Equipment), Wing Fisher, Charlie and Fran Fitzgerald, Lil Gaherty, Bill Gressler, Magdalen Gressler, Arthur Kineke, Little Falls Fire Department, Jimmy Mettot, Bev Kelly and Marietta Phillips (Little Falls Public Library), Peter and Frances Moynihan, Mary Ann Miosek Murphy, Robin Prinzhorn, Pat Ralbovsky, Dolores Restante, Mary Alice Rieman, Sharon Rolchigo, Edward and Gail Rose, Rocco Scarano, Ann Schuyler, Phyllis Shelton, Alan Sterling, Lorraine Heath of *The Times*, Gary Van Veghten, Alan and Linda Vincent, Pauline Walker, Jean Warner, Jean Wolf, Betty Wurzbacher, Gary Zaboly, and Genie Zoller. Thank you to those who shared information for the book: Donald Buckley, Tony Gabriel, Mike Gelfuso (New York State Department of Transportation), pastor Elizabeth Harter, Joseph Lasowski, Michael Liscio, Larry Ortlieb, Ken Rose, Linda Salarpi, Robin Campbell, and John Scarano. Unless otherwise noted, images come from the authors' collections.

INTRODUCTION

Following the retreat of the last ice sheet covering this portion of North America, a huge lake existed between what are now the Great Lakes region and central New York. Thousands of years ago, the Precambrian divide at Little Falls was breached, and outpouring water created a waterfall greater than Niagara Falls, eventually creating the gorge at Little Falls. Bottom-scouring rocks formed the potholes on Moss Island during this geological process. The width of the valley floor suggests the original reach of the Mohawk River.

When the first white traders appeared in the mid-Mohawk Valley region in the late 1600s, they encountered river rapids at a place the Mohawk Indians called *Astenrogan* ("swift water"), where they had to carry their canoes around the Little Falls. They named the area to distinguish it from the Big Falls at Cohoes. A group of Palatine (German) settlers purchased a large tract of land from the Mohawks in 1722, and in 1725, this purchase was validated by the Burnetsfield Patent, which granted 92 persons a trace of land on both sides of the Mohawk River beginning at the Little Falls.

Eventually the carrying place around the rapids became a settlement in the Little Falls area. A gristmill was later constructed. Native American trails and wagon roads became streets, and the area became a Revolutionary War–era buffer between Albany and the frontier. This experience created a greater sense of community. In 1811, the New York State Legislature granted Little Falls a charter, and the settlement became a political entity. In 1895, Little Falls became the only city in Herkimer County. From 1850 to 1852, Little Falls was officially named Rockton.

The transportation era in Little Falls began in the 1790s with the construction of the Western Inland Lock and Navigation Canal on the north side of Mill Street. In 1825, the Erie Canal was opened; it was enlarged in 1841. The river and canal have been a constant source of identity and commerce throughout the city's history. Without the rapids, no settlement would have taken place at this point in the Mohawk Gorge.

The mid-1800s brought railroads to Little Falls and the Mohawk Valley; by the 1890s, multiple railroad lines ran through the entire east-west corridor of New York State. With canals and railroads, greater industry and manufacturing came to Little Falls. Textile mills and paper mills employed thousands at one time. Little Falls thrived as a cheese production and distribution center in the mid- to late 1800s. In later years, Snyder's Bicycle and Allegro Shoes were the largest manufacturers in the city, and Little Falls was the manufacturing hub of the mid-Mohawk Valley. Today the largest industries in Little Falls produce stainless steel tanks, fiberglass goods, and paper and wood products.

Ethnic diversity has characterized Little Falls almost since its earliest days. The original Palatine and English character of the community was diversified by the arrival of various European immigrant groups. "Old" immigrants from northern and western Europe, particularly Ireland and Germany, swelled the community's population in the mid-1800s, and the arrival of "new" immigrants from southern and eastern Europe, particularly Italy, Poland, and the Slovak and Slovenian nations, helped the city to reach its population peak of around 13,000 in 1920. The number and variety of church denominations and schools in Little Falls resulted from this ethnic and religious diversity. The past few decades have seen the city become more ethnically and racially diverse.

In the post–World War II era, industries began to abandon the Northeast for the Sunbelt, and Little Falls has felt the full effect of this decline in recent decades. Revitalization efforts have focused attention on Little Falls' waterfront district, and over the past 20 years, a vibrant commercial district centered on the arts has emerged at Canal Place. Additionally, between the 1970s and the present, the city built a new high school, revitalized its YMCA, tastefully added an addition to its public library, and fully reconstructed Benton Hall Academy.

Newcomers to Little Falls continue to be attracted by the physical beauty of the city, including its rich architectural heritage, its beautiful parks, recreational facilities, and its unique culture and character. The nature and direction of future commercial development in Little Falls continues to generate ongoing debate. Like many other communities in upstate New York, Little Falls is transitioning from a manufacturing center into a residential community. The city school district strives to adjust to Little Falls' changing demographics.

This publication is a pictorial history of the city of Little Falls as captured by a wide array of photographers, both professional and non-professional. It is the intention of the Little Falls Historical Society to have this pictorial history complement its Towards Our Bicentennial writing series, which features original articles authored by a variety of present and former residents as the city celebrates its 200th birthday in 2011.

—The Little Falls Historical Society

One

NOTABLE PEOPLE

NATHANIEL S. BENTON.
Nathaniel Benton (1792–
1869) was prominent in
Herkimer County and
Little Falls political affairs,
having been elected the
village's first president in
1827. He went on to become
a state senator (1828–1831),
Herkimer County's first
judge (1832), and the New
York State secretary of state
(1845–1847). He authored the
area's first annals—*History of
Herkimer County*—in 1856.

ROBERT MACKINNON. Robert MacKinnon (1853–1922) started his career in a knitting mill in Cohoes. He rose through the ranks, formed the firm of Ablett, MacKinnon, and Company in 1881, and came to Little Falls. In 1887, he withdrew from the firm and began the manufacture of knit goods on his own, establishing the MacKinnon Knitting Mills, which became a large employer in Little Falls, on East Mill Street.

ANDREW LITTLE. Born in Scotland, Andrew Little (1837–1935) came to the United States and eventually settled in Little Falls in 1876, when he was hired to do the woodwork for the construction of the Methodist church. Using his carpentry talents, he started a woodworking mill manufacturing all parts of house woodwork in 1892, forming a thriving business, Andrew Little and Sons. Little is pictured to the far right. (Courtesy of LFHS.)

DAVID H. BURRELL. One of Little Falls' most noted citizens, David H. Burrell (1841–1919) began his career selling cheese from the local dairies in New York City with his father, Harry. He partnered with Rodney Whitman to manufacture and sell dairy equipment in 1880. He became the sole owner in 1885 to form the D. H. Burrell Company. In addition to manufacturing dairying equipment, Burrell invented machinery needed to process dairy products. A true civic leader, he donated half of the money to build city hall and built the YMCA building as well as the towering Burrell building. He was instrumental in building the city's public water system. Although he never graduated from an institution of learning, in 1914, Hamilton College conferred on him an honorary degree in recognition of his substantial services rendered to both business and community. (Courtesy of Wing Fisher.)

11

FRANK J. VINCENT. Little Falls native Frank Vincent (1861–1951) began to manufacture mattresses in the city in 1892, erecting a factory on Southern Avenue in 1896. His son, Neely, became a partner and moved the business to West Mill Street in 1952. His grandson Alan Vincent joined the company in 1968. It became the leading supplier of mattress felt to manufacturers in upstate New York. (Courtesy of Alan and Linda Vincent.)

THEODORE ROGERS. The Honorable Theodore Rogers (1880–1940) was a political and business leader in the community. In 1900, he came to Little Falls, where he started working for D. H. Burrell. In 1914, he formed a partnership with Matthew Ashe and built up a flourishing business in insurance and real estate. He served as Republican county chairman for six years and represented the county as member of assembly for four terms from 1925 to 1928.

ANDREW A. BURROWS. The founder of the Burrows Paper Corporation, Andrew (1883–1949) became president and general manager, helping the company grow into one of the leading tissue paper mills in the country. He brought industries to Little Falls as chairman of the Industrial Committee during the Depression, and he was active in church work, serving as the Mohawk District lay leader of the Northern New York Methodist Conference. (Courtesy of Burrows Paper Corporation.)

GEORGE W. GRESSLER. George Gressler (1888–1967), a native of Little Falls, was a "striper" of horse carriages before moving to Elkhart, Indiana, to work in a Studebaker factory. Returning to Little Falls in the 1920s with his bride, Charlotte Adams, he worked as a painting contractor and dance instructor. He served the city as an alderman in the Third Ward. (Courtesy of Bill Gressler.)

PATRICK J. DINNEEN. Patrick Dinneen (1858–1950) was the lamplighter of Little Falls, his job being to adjust the carbons in the gaslit lamps that illuminated the city streets. He would pass out the old carbons to children, who would use it as an early form of sidewalk chalk. He worked for 43 years as an employee of the Central New York Power Corporation and its predecessors. (Courtesy of David Dinneen.)

UTICA GAS AND ELECTRIC COMPANY EMPLOYEES. Electric streetlights replaced gaslit lamps in Little Falls on February 1, 1892. The Utica Gas and Electric Company was founded in 1898. Pictured from left to right in this 1950 photograph are company employees (first row) Adelbert Collins, Dennis Danahy, Bob Manning, and M. Vail Sr.; (second row) Tom Vail, superintendent Charles Walsh, and Clete Kearns Sr.; (third row) Patrick Dinneen and an unidentified employee. (Courtesy of David Dinneen.)

POLICE DEPARTMENT. From 1884 to 1896, Earl Harris was police chief, succeeded by John O'Rourke and later by August Halling. James Long was appointed chief in 1905, serving for 35 years until his retirement in 1940. During his term, police headquarters were moved to the city hall. Francis Reardon was then appointed chief, taking a leave of absence to serve with the navy during World War II. The above picture shows the 1950 Little Falls Police Department. From left to right are (first row) Del Rathbun, Dan Kubica, Chief Francis Reardon, Emil Schwiler, and Nick Hollick; (second row) Paul Riesley, Frank Wnuk, Frank Matus, and Ted Bugaj; (third row) Bernard Miller, Anthony Vallacorsa, Kenneth Travis, Ed Brezdenk, and George O'Neil. The picture below shows a Memorial Day parade in the 1950s. Pictured from left to right are (first row) Chief Reardon, (second row) Charlie Colby, Dan Kubica, Ken Travis, Mike Ashe, Bernard Miller, and Del Rathbun. (Courtesy of LFHS.)

LITTLE FALLS POLICEMEN AROUND 1906. Shown above from left to right are (first row) Chief James "Dusty" Long (1864–1944); (second row) John Dundon, Pat McLaughlin (1868–1957), Capt. Levi Grose (1871–1960), Charles Grose (1868–1939), and Irving Klock. The picture at left features a reflective shot of Chief Long at the end of a 45-year career with the Little Falls Police Department. He first became a policeman the year that Little Falls became a city (1895) and had worked his way to captain by September 3, 1903. On November 1, 1905, Long became the town's chief of police, and he remained at this post until December 31, 1940. During the intervening 35 years, he made Little Falls a city from which criminals found it wise to steer clear. (Courtesy of David Dinneen.)

LITTLE FALLS FIRE DEPARTMENT. The above picture shows the fire department posing with its equipment in front of its quarters in the new city hall building in the winter of 1923. The city's first volunteer fire company was organized on June 6, 1827. By 1899, there were six fire companies with a total membership of 700 men. That year, the city decided to replace the volunteers with a full-time paid fire department. The volunteers continued to work with the paid department to provide the city with fire protection. The lower picture shows the Little Falls call firemen in 1921. From left to right are (first row) Eddie Groffman, Emit Bucklin, Thomas Morse, Amos Clarke, Francis Reardon, and Ed Maguire; (second row) Clarence Smith and George Foley. (Above, courtesy of LFHS; below, courtesy of Little Falls Fire Department.)

THE SLOVAKS. The first Slovak to come to Little Falls was Anna Ragan. Soon after, friends and relatives from Myjava, Slovakia, followed, and as many as 500 to 600 people from that region settled in Little Falls. Identified in this picture, standing in front of a boardinghouse on the south side, are Elizabeth Stibrany (Klimacek), standing at left in a black dress, and Suzanna Stibrany (Malavasic), standing to the right of her sister in a white blouse. (Courtesy of Pauline Walker.)

THE SLOVENIANS. In the late 1890s, people came from Austria-Hungary to live in Little Falls on Danube and Jefferson Streets. By 1905, they formed the St. Joseph's Society, a cultural, social, and beneficial organization that observed special holidays and customs, offered insurance and disability benefits, and taught children the Slovenian language. Pictured is the 55th anniversary of St. Joseph's Society No. 53 on March 19, 1960. (Courtesy of Mary Ann Miosek Murphy.)

SLOVENIAN HOME. In 1911, the community purchased the property of Andrew Spacapan at 36 Danube Street to secure a home for its organization. With several alterations, it served as the Slovenian Home (Hall) for many years. On March 23, 1928, the property interests of the St. Joseph's Society were transferred to the Slovenian Home, and it became incorporated. The group's activities included a fall grape festival, a Slovenian band, and masquerade dances held the first Saturday in Lent. Pictured from left to right are (first row) Herman Schwasnick Sr., Teresa Urh Masle, unidentified, Catherine Lapajne Prestopnik, Mrs. Logar, Helen Masle, Mary Kauchich Hughes, Dorothy Masle Becker, Jane Kauchich Schwasnick, unidentified, and Teresa Turk Gregorka; (second row) Max Miosek, Jane Prestopnik Miosek, Tony Schneider, and Rose Miosek Schneider. The club building was sold in 1984. (Courtesy of Mary Ann Miosek Murphy.)

St. Mary's Ladies Aid Society. The Slovenian residents attended St. Mary's Roman Catholic Church. A ladies aid society was formed consisting of Slovenian women who would plan picnics and parties to raise money to pay sick benefits to its members. Pictured is the "Kitchen Crew" at the Slovenian Hall. From left to right are Theresa Masle, Jenny Silc, Catherine Lapajne Prestopnik, Katy Homovec, Anna Prijatel, and Antonia Prtavs. (Courtesy of Mary Ann Miosek Murphy.)

Training for Navy and Marine Corps, 1944. Shown standing in front of city hall are some of Little Falls' future soldiers and sailors. From left to right, they are (first row) Edwin Vosburg, Stephen Adasek, Ervin Staring, William Hooper, and Andrew Noonan; (second row) Ralph George Jr., Zygmunt Bugaj, and Raymond Andrilla; (third row) John Valuck, Leroy Van Slyke, Martin Krchniak Jr., Albert Trask Jr., Anthony George, and Carl Taylor. (Courtesy of LFHS.)

LITTLE FALLS BOY SCOUT TROOP 51. Camp Russell on White Lake was donated to the Boy Scout Association by Samuel T. Russell of Ilion, and Boy Scouts from all over the area have been enjoying their summers there for years. Shown here is Boy Scout Troop No. 51 of Little Falls at Camp Russell. From left to right are (first row) Bill Moynihan, Dave Edwards, Dave Malone, B. Frazier, Lenard Federico, Nick Sanzo, Ted Creeden, Harry Balderton, David O'Connor, Peter Balderston, L. VanKernan, and Greg Beasley; (second row) Stan Bonk, John Ashe, Joe Vail, Pete Day, Jerry Sullivan, Tom Toher, John Gillen, Bill Nash, H. Palinski, and Gary Beasley; (third row) Joe Lambert, J. Jorig, Neil Baum, William Van Allen, John Cooney, Robert Long, and Denis Sivack; (fourth row) N. J. Sanzo and Scoutmaster Francis Ashe. (Courtesy of Camp Russell.)

WILBUR CRISP. Coach "Bull" Crisp (1891–1969), a longtime educator and sports figure, began his career as a standout basketball player at Syracuse University. He moved to Little Falls in 1926 to teach physical education and coach a winning basketball team, compiling a career of 334 wins against 167 losses. He led Little Falls to the New York State Championship in the 1929–1930 season. He invented basketball and wrestling scoring books and the first electric basketball timer. The high school gymnasium was named in his honor in 1967. In 2002, he was inducted into the Basketball Coaches Association of New York's Hall of Fame. Crisp is seen second from left accepting a trophy, along with coach Charles Fitzgerald of St. Mary's Academy. On the far left is Principal George Cummings. At far right is Rev. Harold Thomson. (Courtesy of Fran Fitzgerald.)

MR. AND MRS. LOOMIS BURRELL.
Loomis Burrell (1872–1975) and
his wife, Lois Watson Wing (1887–
1973), were both scientists, together
developing chlorine sterilizers for
use in sanitizing dairy equipment.
Loomis joined his father at D. H.
Burrell and Company, where he
developed a cream separator and
perfected milking machines. When
the company changed to Cherry-
Burrell Corporation, he became its
first chairman. He was president
of Herkimer County Trust from
1941 to 1948. Their daughter,
Wing Fisher (below), graduated
from Vassar College (1934) and
became involved in banking.
In 1971, she was one of the first
women to serve as a director for
Herkimer County Trust, following a
family line starting with her great-
grandfather Arphaxed Loomis.
She was trustee of the Little Falls
Hospital from the mid-1950s
until 1995, serving as president
(1978–1980) and as a longtime
trustee at Little Falls Public Library.
(Courtesy of Wing Fisher.)

DOROTHY RICHARDS. Dorothy (Burney) Richards (1894–1985) established Beaversprite, a sanctuary for beavers and other wildlife in the town of Oppenheim. Dorothy and her husband, Allison, were Little Falls natives. After living in Canada and Albany, they returned to Little Falls in 1930 and purchased an office supply firm, renaming it A. M. Richards Supply Company. They also purchased property in Fulton County. When state officials asked them to keep two beavers there, Beaversprite began in 1932. Dorothy had the beavers as visitors in her home, where they were fed and practically domesticated. She donated her 900-acre property to the Florence Erdmann Trust to assure that it would remain forever wild. The sanctuary grew to 1,300 acres, and a nature center was developed. Richards's activities attracted national attention when she appeared on NBC's *Real People*. (Courtesy of Beavers, Wetlands, and Wildlife.)

DR. BERNARD BURKE. Dr. Burke (1916–1998) reminds one of the country doctor normally found only in books and films. After serving in World War II, he came to Little Falls, where he quickly became a staple at Little Falls Hospital. In the years that followed, he delivered over 5,000 babies and tended all sorts of ills, often without charging for his services. His caring ways are memorialized in all of the sites dedicated to him: the Benton Hall Academy Library, Burke Park (formerly Western), and Bernard J. Burke Memorial Highway. Sadly, twice in his later years, he became the focus of restrictions placed on his practice by the state. While the public rallied each time to his cause, he quietly continued his practice, within the state's constraints. He loved being a family doctor, and he was one in the truest sense of the profession. (Courtesy of Benton Hall Academy.)

ARNOLD BLUMBERG. Arnold Blumberg (1896–1978) was a noted Little Falls businessman, politician, and judge. He served as city attorney from 1925 to 1927, at which time he became children's court judge for Herkimer County until 1934. Blumberg was also a director of the Little Falls National Bank (1934–1978) and a director of the Building Savings and Loan Association from 1934 to 1973.

HON. BERNARD MALONE. Judge Malone (1915–2003) was admitted to the bar in 1939 and founded the law firm of Malone and Malone, practicing with sons David and Robert and daughter-in-law Joy. He took office as city judge in 1946, serving 25 years. He was the first World War II veteran to serve as commander of American Legion Post No. 31 and was a member of the Elks Lodge No. 42, and director of Little Falls National Bank. (Courtesy of LFHS.)

ZAIDA ZOLLER. The founder of the Herkimer County Humane Society in 1913, Zaida Zoller (1882–1980) had a deep devotion to animals and remained active in the society all of her life. She was a leader in the woman's suffrage movement, championing the rights for women to vote during World War I. She received the S.Sgt. Steve Stefula Post No. 4612 Little Falls VFW Citizenship Award in 1957. (Courtesy of Genie Zoller.)

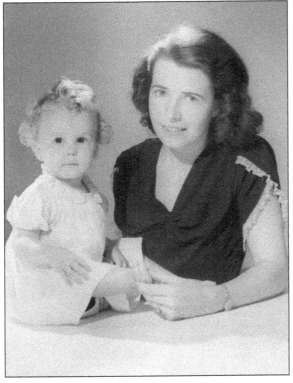

CAROLYN ZOLLER. "Chiqua" Zoller (1912–2003), with daughter Susie, was a granddaughter of U.S. senator Warner Miller of Herkimer. She married John Zoller in 1940, moving to Little Falls. She gave generously of her time to many organizations, being a member of the DAR Astenrogen Chapter and Herkimer County Historical Society for more than 50 years. She organized a children's group of the DAR, served on the Mohawk Homestead Board, and authored *Mohawk Valley Zollers.* (Courtesy of Genie Zoller.)

MARY HAGGERTY. Mary Haggerty (1948–2006) was Little Falls' own Jill-of-all-civic-trades. A native of the city, she was first and foremost an educator, teaching in Little Falls schools for 34 years. She devoted her life to helping people. Her longest service was to the Foothills Girl Scout Council, in which she served as troop leader, national convention delegate, day camp director, and first-aid trainer for leaders. Mary was also active in the American Red Cross and was a disaster chairperson who served personally after Hurricanes Hugo and Katrina and the 9/11 catastrophe. In her spare time, she served on the board of the Women's Christian Association, the Little Falls Historical Society, Little Falls Hospital Guild, and the Astenrogen Chapter of the DAR. In 2007, Girl Scout troops from Little Falls honored her with memorial benches overlooking Benton Hall. (Courtesy of Mohawk Valley Red Cross.)

HANK BROWN. Shown here with Phil Rizzuto, former Yankee shortstop and announcer, Hank is celebrating over 50 years as a radio personality. He reaches over 1.8 million listeners in upstate New York and Canada with the *Hank Brown Show.* His down-home manner makes him seem like a personal friend. He was the boxing-ring announcer at the 1996 Summer Olympics and became the voice of USA Boxing. He is the emcee at the Boxing Hall of Fame (since 1990) and Baseball Hall of Fame (since 1957) and announces for the Empire State Games (since 1960). Throughout his career, Hank has worked with television personalities from musicians to professional athletes. Readers may remember his local television dance show *Twist-A-Rama,* which premiered on November 1, 1964, with guest Neil Sedaka. It became the highest-rated local television show in the country. (Courtesy of Esther Brown.)

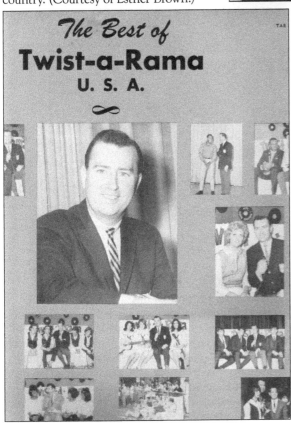

JOHN RICCARDO. John Riccardo, son of Peter and Mary Riccardo, had a choice of working in one of the local factories or getting an education after graduating from Little Falls High School in 1942. He chose the latter, graduating from the University of Michigan with bachelor's (1949) and master's (1950) degrees. Riccardo joined Chrysler Corporation in 1959 as a financial staff manager. The next year, he was already being promoted to general manager of the Export-Import Division, and in 1961, he was named vice president of Chrysler Canada, Ltd. He continued to take on positions of authority in the company until elected president of the Chrysler Corporation in January 1970. Riccardo hired Lee Iacocca as Chrysler president in 1978; ten months later, Riccardo resigned, and Iacocca was elected chairman of the corporation. (Courtesy of LFHS.)

Two

NOTABLE EVENTS

GULF CURVE TRAIN WRECK. New York Central's Lake Shore Limited derailed on the Little Falls Gulf Curve on the night of April 19, 1940, leaving 31 people dead and 100 injured. It was the third-deadliest wreck in the 20th century. The train was traveling west from Albany to Chicago, Illinois. A stone monument was placed near the site of the wreck in 1990.

ATTRACTS MANY ONLOOKERS. The train wreck was caused when the engineer maneuvered the sharp gulf curve at too high a rate of speed, derailing it from the tracks. The terrible tragedy brought out large numbers of people to view its aftermath, and many photographs were taken—including this one.

WELCOME HOME PARADE, 1946. On July 4, 1946, the city welcomed home the veterans with a parade and special ceremonies in Eastern Park. Special guest Gov. Thomas Dewey sits in the front center of the large crowd. He spoke after the parade and presented Dr. Augustus Santry with an award for his faithful service to the draft boards in both world wars. (Courtesy of LFHS.)

LITTLE FALLS SESQUICENTENNIAL. During the week of July 22–29, 1961, a huge celebration commemorated the 150th anniversary of Little Falls' incorporation. Mayor John W. George oversaw the week's events with celebration chairman Dr. Fred Sabin. The event kicked off with a huge parade with at least 25,000 people lined along the route, which took over two hours to traverse. The grand marshal was Alton C. Millen. The lower picture shows the New York Telephone float with a princess telephone on the front. Riding on the float were telephone employees Ann Murphy Billings (left), Magdalen Kohn Gressler (right), and Eleanor Grande Karpowich (back). (Above, courtesy of LFHS; below, courtesy of Magdalen Gressler.)

HISTORICAL PAGEANT. *Shadows of Yesteryear*, a historical pageant depicting events in the history of Little Falls was presented on the evenings of July 25–29 at Veterans Memorial Park. The pageant was produced by the John B. Rogers Company with a local cast. Historian Edward Cooney assisted with the history and research for the pageant, as well as editing a historical souvenir booklet for the event. (Courtesy of LFHS.)

THE BROWN FAMILY. Everyone commemorated the city's early days by wearing authentic old-time attire for the event's activities. Pictured here is the emcee for many of the events, local radio personality Hank Brown. With him are his wife, Esther, and their daughters, (left to right) Eileen, Cathleen, and Colleen. (Courtesy of Esther Brown.)

BROTHERS OF THE BRUSH. There were 41 chapters organized for Brothers of the Brush, including one for the Lock Tavern on River Road, pictured here. The committee that helped organize the Brothers of the Brush consisted of chairman Edward Pawluk and Dave Dunn, Floyd Houck, Stan Kukowski, Nicholas Staffo, Walter Viparina, and Walter Walrath. (Courtesy of Janet Crimmins.)

CELEBRATION BELLES. Local women organized their own chapter of Celebration Belles; 33 chapters consisted of 898 members. Lock Tavern was home to the "Lockettes," pictured here. The Belles' cochairs were Helen Clifford and Dorothy Muhl. Pauline Martinovic was chair of ladies' participation. (Courtesy of Janet Crimmins.)

WHISKER-JUDGING CONTEST. On the afternoon of July 29, the eve of the sesquicentennial celebration, the Brothers of the Brush participated in a whisker-judging contest in Eastern Park. That evening, the men went to the pageant site at Veterans Park for a "shave-off" sponsored by Remington-Rand. Pictured above are some of the pre-shorn men with the Sesquicentennial Court. From left to right are (first row) Barbara Steele Connor, Fred Staring Sr., Frank Ferjanec, Sesquicentennial queen Karen Carpenter Lorenzoni, Harold Thomas, and Kay Donovan Guiney; (second row) Ed Sherman, Dan Bennett, unidentified, and Tony Gabriel. The lower picture shows the men in the midst of shaving. From left to right are (first row) Fred Staring Sr., Frank Ferjanec, Harold Thomas, Kay Donovan Guiney, Karen Carpenter Lorenzoni, and mayor John George; (second row) Ed Sherman, Dan Bennett, unidentified, and Tony Gabriel. (Courtesy of LFHS.)

ANNUAL THANKSGIVING DAY PARADE. Little Falls held a Thanksgiving Day parade to kick off the holiday season. Afterwards, children would head to the Rialto Theatre to enjoy free movies and popcorn. Santa Claus would make his entrance on the stage and hand out boxes of candy before sending the kids out the side door to their waiting parents. The above picture, taken in the late 1950s, shows the Little Falls High School band walking on Albany Street. Of the buildings shown here, the only one left today is the Little Falls Historical Museum, in the far back. The rest were razed; the site is now the M&T Bank parking lot. The picture below shows a North Ann Street apartment building (now a parking lot for Xtra-Mart) and Lawrence Gallagher's home (now Stewart's). (Courtesy of *The Times*.)

URBAN RENEWAL. In 1958, the U.S. government approved Little Falls for an urban renewal program. Phase I involved the clearing of buildings on East Main Street in the heart of the business district for an attractive shopping plaza and a new senior citizen housing complex on John Street. Construction began in 1964 and was completed in 1969. The above picture shows West John Street and West Main Street coming to a point, as they originally did before urban renewal. The new Route 5 highway had not been built yet. The lower picture shows the demolition of old buildings on the corner of Ann and Main Streets, including Trasks Cigar Store, Clemens Drug store, Ackerman's Clothing, and Eddie's Tavern. The new Herkimer County Trust complex was built in its place. (Courtesy of *The Times*.)

NEW ARTERIAL HIGHWAY. Phase II of urban renewal involved the state highway department's construction of a four-lane arterial highway for Route 5 (shown above), designed to help alleviate downtown traffic congestion and allow the Main Street business district to be redeveloped as a modern shopping center. Sections of West John, West Main, and Hancock Streets had to be removed. The picture below shows the intersection where West John Street met West Main Street near Furnace Street. The old factory buildings being demolished are Snyder's, Little Falls Felt Shoe, and Gilbert's. The site is now home to Tri-County Medical. (Courtesy of *The Times*.)

HILLARY CLINTON VISIT. Senatorial candidate and former first lady Hillary Clinton visited Little Falls on February 10, 2000. She is pictured with local residents (left to right) Mary Darman, Mary Girmonde, and Ann Blask. Clinton went on to win two terms as senator from New York. She conducted an unsuccessful run for U.S. president and is currently U.S. secretary of state. (Courtesy of Ann Blask.)

ERIE CANAL CORRIDOR GRANTS. On August 18, 1999, from left to right, congressman Sherwood Boehlert, mayor Craig Hebert, and City of Little Falls Urban Renewal Agency administrator Mark Feane joined HUD secretary Andrew Cuomo for a grant presentation to Little Falls to promote the Erie Canal Corridor. Cuomo's tour highlighted the area's historic, cultural, and recreational attractions, including travel by boat, bike, and road from Buffalo to Albany. (Courtesy of Ann Blask.)

Three

HISTORIC HOMES
AND BUILDINGS

HERKIMER COUNTY BANK. The first bank in the county was incorporated in 1833 and started in a room at the Beattie House. Later that year, it moved to this building at Ann and Albany Streets, which served as a bank until 1917. The Little Falls Historical Society started the process of obtaining the building in 1970 and moved their headquarters here in 1977. It is on the National Register of Historic Places. (Courtesy of LFHS.)

BELLINGER TAVERN. This Colonial brick house, located on Route 5S southeast of Little Falls, was built as a tavern in the 1820s by John C. Bellinger (1793–1881). In 1882, the property was purchased by Henry Bellinger and used as a residence. His grandson, James Bellinger, inherited the property and operated a creamery and dairy farm with his son, Raymond.

WCA. The Women's Christian Academy (WCA), at 534 Garden Street, was originally built around 1830 as a home for Judge Nathaniel Benton (1792–1869). Benton's wife continued to reside there until her death in 1881. In 1920, the Burrell family purchased the home to give to the people of Little Falls for the WCA. It opened on November 22, 1920, and was dedicated to the memory of Anne Louise Burrell. (Courtesy of LFHS.)

BOYER HOME. This *c.* 1857 brick residence at 49 Jackson Street was built by well-known contractor Joseph Boyer (1814–1874), builder of the Skinner Opera House. In 1881, the house was sold to John Satterlee (1791–1877), proprietor of a paper mill. Elmer Mulford, who ran the Cheney Hammer Company, resided there from the 1930s to the 1970s. Today it is the home of Keith and Marion Davy. (Courtesy of LFHS.)

HARDIN MANSION. George Anson Hardin (1832–1901) built this impressive home at 512 East Gansevoort Street. Elected as state senator in 1861, Hardin also served as Herkimer County district attorney and New York State Supreme Court judge. He authored his *History of Herkimer County* in 1893. The house was razed in 1938 and is now the site of Holy Trinity Lutheran Church. (Courtesy of LFHS.)

BRAMER HOME. Frank Bramer (1834–1888) came to Little Falls from Massachusetts to become manager of the Warrior Mower Company. His mansard-roofed brick home on the corner of East Main Street and Waverly Place was built in 1876. Bramer's daughter Nellie (1864–1906) married county judge Rollin Smith (1838–1911) who inherited the home. Judge Smith, in his will, deeded the home to the city for use as a public library and provided an endowment for its conversion. Mabel Richards oversaw the building's renovation into a library and served devotedly as its librarian until ill health forced her retirement a few years before her death in 1974. In 1982, a new addition was built and dedicated. The old section now houses reading, reference, and storage rooms, while the addition contains the main library and community rooms. (Courtesy of Little Falls Public Library.)

BURCH HOME. Built in the early 1830s by Horace Burch (1811–1895) at 48 North Ann Street, it remained in the family until 1937. Burch built up a mercantile business on the corner of Second and Main Streets that was considered the largest dry goods dealer in central New York. In 1945, the home was purchased by Ford Trask (1909–1966), owner of Little Falls Wholesale Company. In the 1970s, it was operated as St. Joseph's Home for the Aged. The home has undergone major renovations to its exterior and is currently owned by Edward and Gail Rose. (Courtesy of Edward and Gail Rose.)

ZOLLER HOME. Jacob Zoller (1833–1907) completed this Venetian-Gothic brick house in 1879. He was a cheese broker, selling for 50 cheese factories. In 1883, Zoller built a warehouse on Mill Street. He was a pioneer in food processing, opening a cold-storage plant in 1894. The home has stayed in the family as a residence for daughters Maude and Zaida and as the law office of grandson John Zoller.

LOOMIS HOUSE. This 1832 home at 676 East Main Street was the residence of Arphaxed Loomis (1792–1886). It remains in the family today, occupied by great-granddaughter Wing Fisher. Loomis served as president of the village and was a county and surrogate judge, congressman, and assemblyman. Through his efforts, the Ellice property was sold in 1831, assisting the growth of Little Falls. (Courtesy of Wing Fisher.)

OVERLOOK MANSION. This castle-like residence was designed by Archimedes Russell and built by David H. Burrell in 1889. It has 26 rooms, a small self-contained hydroelectric plant, an elevator, an indoor swimming pool, and a bowling alley. In 1885, Burrell founded the D. H. Burrell Company, which developed and manufactured dairy equipment. In 1994, Armando and Carin Mei operated it as a restaurant and bed-and-breakfast. Today it is privately owned. (Courtesy of Wing Fisher.)

HOMER P. SNYDER HOME. This was the home of Homer P. Snyder (1863–1937), located at the corner of Lansing and North Ann Streets. In 1898, Snyder formed the H. P. Snyder Manufacturing Company, which became the largest distributor of bicycles and velocipedes in the world. He also served the community as a U.S. congressman from 1914 to 1925. Today his former home is the law office of Blumberg and Carrig. (Courtesy of LFHS.)

GILBERT MANSION. Seen here shortly after its completion, this beautiful home with a red-tiled roof at 36 Prospect Street was built around 1915 by Joshua Judson Gilbert (1861–1925), founder of the Gilbert Knitting Company. When Joshua's widow, Margaret, died in 1962, the home went to their daughter, Esther, and their son-in-law, Arthur Van der Gracht, who became president of the company. (Courtesy of LFHS.)

CHAPMAN-MOSER FUNERAL HOME. This house at 42 North Ann Street was built in 1854 by George Ashley, owner of the village's first hardware store. Walter Becker (1874–1956) purchased the house before World War I. He organized Little Falls Fibre Company in 1904. The home was purchased in 1958 by Floyd Chapman, who renovated it for use as a mortuary. In 1984, it became the Chapman-Moser Funeral Home. (Courtesy of LFHS.)

DR. SHARER HOME. This home at 634 East John Street was home to two of the city's longtime physicians. Dr. John Sharer (1824–1899) opened his practice in Little Falls in 1848. Besides keeping a private medical practice, he was also the physician-in-charge at Stafford's Gold Cure Institute. The house was later occupied by Dr. George Eveleth (1865–1957), who practiced medicine in the city from 1892 until he retired in 1954. (Courtesy of LFHS.)

FISHER HOME. This home at 28 Waverly Place was built in 1896 by Michael Fisher (1866–1927), partner of Homer Snyder in the manufacture of knitting machines and bicycles. The next year, he moved to Fort Plain to start his own business and sold the house to the MacKinnon family. It was later sold to George Smith; his widow, Inez, lived there until her death in 1973. Today it is the residence of Burrell and Martha Fisher. (Courtesy of LFHS.)

RODNEY WHITMAN HOME. Rodney Whitman (1834–1918) built this Queen Anne–style redbrick home on the corner of Ann and West Gansevoort Streets in 1898. He conducted the Rockton knitting mill on Mohawk Street. After his widow, Elizabeth, passed in 1943, the house was vacant, and the local Elks lodge purchased the building in 1945 on the lodge's 59th anniversary. (Courtesy of LFHS.)

SAMUEL WHITMAN HOME. Samuel Whitman (1804–1877) came to Little Falls with his wife, Mary Arnold, in 1839. They built this home at 2 West Monroe Street. Samuel was a farmer and agent for Bullard Hay Tedders. After Mary's death in 1892, the house was used for a kindergarten school operated by Laura Jenks, who graduated from a kindergarten training school in New York City. Visible in the background of this photograph are homes at 72 and 74 Diamond Street. (Courtesy of LFHS.)

KINDERGARTEN CLASS. This *c.* 1895 photograph features a class of kindergartners at the Whitman home. Shown from left to right are (first row) Nellis Bronner, Fletcher Smith, William Little, and Mary Searles Wicks; (second row) Helen Wheeler Shaper, Marguerite McKinnon, Floyd Van Valkenburg, Paul Merriott, Carrie Casler McEwen, James Bronner, and Gordon Little; (third row) Ethel Timmerman Courow, Isabel McKinnon, Rugene Walrath, Estelle Snyder Teall, Walter Randall Whitman, Grace Burney Schermerhorn, Marie Smith, and Peter Ingham. (Courtesy of LFHS.)

GOWEN HOME. The Fred Gowen (1857–1921) home at 556 East Gansevoort Street is decorated for the Fourth of July in this 1912 photograph. Gowen came to Little Falls in 1886 and operated a grocery store on the corner of Main and Mary Streets. He later traveled the country as a salesman for the H. A. Moyer Company of Syracuse, a wagon manufacturer.

YMCA. The Young Men's Christian Association (YMCA) building on Jackson Street opened on January 14, 1913. Little Falls' first YMCA was incorporated in 1883 but went defunct in 1890. Some 20 years later, David H. Burrell proposed the formation of a citizens' association to benefit the "Christian civilization of the community" and funded the construction of what was first called the Presbyterian Parish House. The title and name were later changed, and a new YMCA was incorporated; it still serves the city today. The c. 1927 picture below shows a group of boys ready to head to the YMCA camp at Fourth Lake. This camp gave many of the city's children a chance to spend some time each summer in the wilds of the Adirondacks. (Courtesy of LFHS.)

MASONIC TEMPLE. The cornerstone of the Little Falls Masonic Temple was laid in 1914 at the corner of Prospect and School Streets, and the finished building was dedicated on June 19, 1915. The Little Falls Lodge No. 181 was organized on September 17, 1849, and continued to serve the city until it was merged with Dolgeville Lodge No. 796 in 2003. Built in a French Medieval style, this impressive building also housed Freemasonry's concordant bodies: the Royal Arch Masonry, Knights Templar, Order of the Eastern Star, and Junior Stars. The interior was finished with fine oak woodwork. The lodge room was most impressive, furnished with oak paneling and built-in bench seating along its walls. A raised dais and carved-oak covering accented the master's seat. The large rock across Church Street from the temple holds a bronze plaque and marks the site of the Octagon Church. (Courtesy of LFHS.)

CITY HALL. In 1914, the construction of a city hall was undertaken with the backing of David H. Burrell, who offered $50,000 if the city would raise the same amount. Land at the southeast corner of Main and William Streets was purchased the next year. The contract was awarded to the George Wills Company, and the building was completed in 1918. The fire department was the first to move in, followed by the police department, city clerk, treasurer, board of public works, and other branches of Little Falls' city government. Incorporated in 1895 as a city, the governing body was first known as the city legislature and was later renamed the common council. The picture above shows the legislative chambers. The body met there for the first time on December 23, 1918. (Courtesy of LFHS.)

Four

CHURCHES

OCTAGON CHURCH.
Construction on
Little Falls' first
church started in
1794. Difficulties
between the various
congregations of this
"union" church and
lack of funding delayed
its completion until the
early 1800s. As each
denomination that
occupied the structure
outgrew the facilities,
it erected its own
building and vacated
the little church. The
structure became
known as the Octagon
Church because
of its unique eight-
sided construction.

LITTLE FALLS FIRST PRESBYTERIAN CHURCH.
Local Presbyterians sought to organize their own separate church in 1812. In 1831, the congregation bought lots on the corner of Albany and Ann Streets and built a brick church, incorporating as the First Presbyterian Society. This church was enlarged over the years and had a seating capacity of 400. The last services were held here on February 29, 1880. (Courtesy of Ann Schuyler.)

NEW CHURCHES BUILT. The new Gothic- and Queen Anne–style Presbyterian church was dedicated on Jackson Street on April 27, 1881. Its was built to conform to the acute angle created by the intersection of Jackson and Lansing Streets. This church was razed in 1973, and the congregation met at the Universalist church while its present church building was erected. It was dedicated in 1975.

Rev. J. Harold Thomson. At the pulpit of the Presbyterian church from 1929 to 1969 was Rev. J. Harold Thomson, a World War I veteran and 1923 graduate of the Princeton Theological Seminary. His roots stemmed back to the area through his mother, Estella Timmerman. A Manheim native, Estella met his father, Rev. John Thomson, while he was a student pastor at the Snells Bush Church.

First Baptist Church of Little Falls. A Baptist congregation was organized in Little Falls in 1829. Meeting at members' homes or the Octagon Church, it was incorporated in December 1830. A church building was started on the corner of Albany and Mary Streets and dedicated on March 31, 1832. It was enlarged in 1858 and again in 1876, when the old steeple was replaced with twin towers.

57

EXTENSIVE RENOVATIONS. In 1968, the First Baptist Church of Little Falls was extensively remodeled. The gymnasium was converted into a fellowship hall and five new Sunday School rooms were added, along with a church office and pastor's study. In 1970, the congregation purchased a 60-passenger bus to transport children to Sunday school; in 1973, it hired a youth pastor to strengthen the church's outreach. Pictured here is the present-day sanctuary. (Courtesy of Arthur Kineke.)

FRANCIS BELLAMY. The original author of the Pledge of Allegiance, Francis Bellamy (1855–1931) was ordained for the ministry on December 14, 1879, at the First Baptist Church of Little Falls, serving as the church's pastor from 1879 to 1885. A plaque on the outside of the church notes Bellamy's ministry there, and a park dedicated in 1959 at the intersection of Gansevoort, Burwell, and Salisbury Streets contains a monument to the clergyman. (Courtesy of *The Times*.)

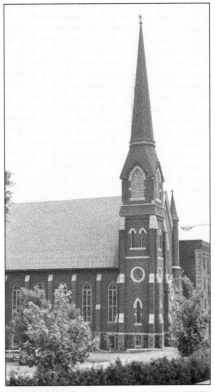

LITTLE FALLS UNITED METHODIST CHURCH.
The town's Methodists shared in the use of the
Octagon Church and officially incorporated a
local Methodist society in 1832. On December
13, 1837, a building committee was formed, and a
lot was secured on Third Street. The church was
dedicated on September 28, 1839, and the last
services were held there on August 1, 1876. A new
Gothic church on Albany Street was dedicated
on August 3, 1876. A gallery reached around
three sides in the sanctuary, which also featured
gaslights and stained-glass windows. Andrew
Little built the stairs leading to the balcony. In
1887, a bell was placed in the belfry. The church
held its last service on October 28, 1990. (Below,
courtesy of Herkimer Methodist Church.)

St. Mary's Catholic Church. Little Falls' Roman Catholic parish was formed around 1833 by missionaries from Utica. In 1847, a frame church was built on John Street. After this burned in 1866, a brick church was built at Alexander and Petrie Streets. The building was found to be structurally unsafe, and construction began in 1874 at the church's present location at East Main and John Streets. The new building was first used on Christmas Day, 1879. A steeple and chimes were added in 1901, and extensive improvements were made to the church's interior in 1914 and 1915. The picture below shows the October 7, 1950, wedding of George and Mary Alice Rieman. Today the church is known as Holy Family Parish. (Above, courtesy of LFHS; below, courtesy of Mary Alice Rieman.)

St. Mary's Academy and Convent. Workers used Little Falls stone to construct a Catholic school in 1889. In 1903, a modern convent for the Sisters of St. Joseph was constructed beside it. Though a 1911 addition nearly doubled the school's size, the high school closed in 1970, and K-8 classes ceased in 1988. From left to right, this overhead view shows the church, the convent, and St. Mary's Academy. (Courtesy of LFHS.)

Sacred Heart Roman Catholic Church. This parish was started as a mission of St. Joseph's Church in Herkimer. The congregation worshipped in a basement church built in 1911 and 1912. A new church was built on the same foundation and dedicated in 1956. A large stained-glass window depicting the Good Shepherd was destroyed in a 1981 fire. The church merged with the two other Catholic parishes in 1991 to establish Holy Family Parish.

St. Joseph's Church. In 1923, St. Joseph's was founded to serve the Italian Catholic community. The first church, at the corner of John and Mary Streets, was destroyed by fire in 1937; parishioners undertook the building of a new brick church at the corner of Albany and William Streets in 1938. In 1991, St. Joseph's was closed, and its parishioners became part of the newly formed Holy Family Parish. Today the former St. Joseph's church building serves as the Little Falls Community Co-op.

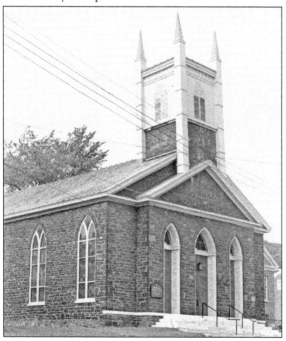

Emmanuel Episcopal Church. Built in 1833 and completed in 1835 on the corner of South William and Albany Streets, Emmanuel was enlarged in 1867, and a chancel was added. On October 27, 1869, the church was reconsecrated. The bell that occupies the stone tower dates back to 1686 in Spain. After the bell was torn from its tower to furnish metal for cannons, pious sailors brought it to New York, where it was purchased by a friend of the parish.

St. Paul's Universalist Church. The St. Paul's congregation formed in 1851. In 1865, it purchased a lot on the corner of Mary and Albany Streets, and a cornerstone was laid on August 1, 1867. In 1908, a new pipe organ was installed in the front of the church, and the choir loft in the rear was converted into a seating gallery. In 1948, many improvements were made, including the restructuring of its steeple to its current height. The picture above shows the church's choir at Easter in 1935 or 1936. Seated in front is organist Edith Woodruff. From left to right, the choir members shown here are (first row) Ann (Kane) Kazmerski, Marilyn Eaker, Eleanor (Roberts) Connolly, Greta (Johnson) Krupa, Mary (Kane) Riemann, Shirley Crocker, Gloria (Billings) Ortlieb, Gladys (Billings) Van Gorder, Betty (Roberts) Marino, Margaret (Miller) Bialock, Bessie Clifford, Mary Irving, and Edith (Phillips) Walrath; (second row) Richard McAllister, Charles Phillips, Marshall Snyder, Grant Phillips, Robert Stewart, and Rev. Howard Gilman. (Courtesy of St. Paul's Unitarian and Universalist Church.)

Tom Thumb Wedding at St. Paul's Universalist Church, 1944. From left to right, the children shown here are (first row) bridesmaids Janice Miller and Carol Povec, best man David Jones, ring-bearer Jack Haefy, groom Bruce Waters, bride Deanna Hall, train-bearer Marlene Kuehnle, flower girls Rhodonna Hall and Ellen Phillips, relative Beverly Pileggi (behind the flower girls), soloist Josephine Kuehnle, and relative Veronica Callister; (second row) Jeanne Fox, Sheila Desmond, and Jean Haefy, usher Joseph Donnelly, maid of honor Deanna Bailey, usher Michael Dedla, minister Dick Kuehnle, mother-of-the-groom Nancy Donnelly, mother-of-the-bride Nancy Gibbs, and father-of-the-bride Teddy Billings. (Courtesy of Pat Ralbovsky, St. Paul's Unitarian and Universalist Church.)

CHRIST LUTHERAN CHURCH. The church was established on August 5, 1900. The congregation purchased the old armory building on Petrie Street, and Rev. Carl Schroeder, pastor of the German Lutheran Church of Herkimer, came to Little Falls to become Christ Lutheran's first minister. Part of the old armory was used in the construction of the church building, which was dedicated on May 27, 1906.

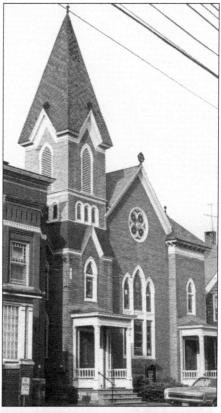

CHRIST LUTHERAN CHURCH PICNIC. Pictured here is a large gathering of church members enjoying a summer picnic. Until the 1940s, services were held in both English and German. The church today is serviced by ordained supply pastors from the synod, and a deacon oversees the church. A section of the old armory building is used for Sunday school and fellowship rooms. (Courtesy of Betty Wurzbacher.)

SLOVAK HOLY TRINITY LUTHERAN CHURCH. The need for a ministry so Slovak immigrants could have services in their own language was first discussed in 1901 at a meeting of the Slovak Evangelical Union. A congregation was formally organized in 1903, when land was acquired for a church cemetery. Stephen Kovara was elected the first lay president of the congregation, and the name Holy Trinity was adopted. Slovak pastors came to the parish from other communities, and the German Lutheran congregation assisted them. The property for the church on East Jefferson Street was purchased in 1907, and in 1912, actual construction of the church began. The building was dedicated on May 18, 1913. The first pastor was Rev. Paul Putra. The picture below shows a funeral procession leaving the church. (Courtesy of LFHS.)

New Church on Gansevoort Street. In 1962, a new parsonage was built on East Monroe Street, and in 1975, a new church was built directly behind it at 512 East Gansevoort Street. The modern design features a two-barred cross at the front and is of frame construction with a brick front panel. The East Jefferson Street church was dedicated on November 23, 1975, as the Assembly of God. (Courtesy of LFHS.)

South Side Union Church. This non-sectarian church was dedicated on May 9, 1903, on East Jefferson Street. It was started in 1890 as Bethel Mission by the YMCA and was devoted to religious charitable works. David H. Burrell funded its construction. One of its ministers was Henry MacIlravy, Chester Gillette's spiritual advisor. The church was razed in 1909 when the Barge Canal was constructed. (Courtesy of LFHS.)

St. Nicholas Ukrainian Orthodox Church. By 1906, Ukrainian immigrants began to settle in Little Falls, and they started building a church on Upper Furnace Street in 1911, completing it the next year. It was an oasis for these immigrants, who felt alone after being driven from their native land by social, economic, and political oppression. Visiting priests looked after the parish until 1960, when a resident priest was appointed.

Ukrainian Church Interior. This picture shows the interior of the church and several members of the congregation before the church closed in 2005. Pictured from left to right are Katherine Merena, Olga Urich, Olga Pelise, Anna Holod, and Jean Warner. (Courtesy of Jean Warner.)

HOLY SPIRIT POLISH NATIONAL
CATHOLIC CHURCH. In the 1920s, about
100 Polish American families lived in
Little Falls. The first organizational
meeting to form a Polish parish was held
in 1926 at Henry Wiernicki's tailor shop.
The church was officially incorporated
on May 20, 1926. In November 1926,
the congregation purchased the redbrick
Lutheran church at 618 Gansevoort
Street. Classes in the Polish language
were taught at the church as well as
religious classes. The parish celebrates
mass in English today, but its choir still
sings many traditional Polish hymns.
In 1926, the parish established its own
cemetery on the north side of Route 5 in
Herkimer. The picture at right shows the
young parish around 1927; the picture
below shows a Confirmation class in
1962. Fr. Josiniski Jabinski stands in
front at the far right. (Courtesy of Holy
Spirit Polish National Catholic Church.)

PAINES HOLLOW CHURCH. In 1840, following a stirring revival, local residents discussed the feasibility of establishing a community church. They dedicated a church building under the name "The Ecclesiastical Society of Paines Hollow" the next year on land donated by Philip Swift Sr. The Reverend James Richards, riding in the Methodist circuit, conducted services every other Sunday, gaining many converts. It became a Methodist church and chartered as the Methodist Protestant Church of Paines Hollow in 1883. Today the church stands conspicuously at the crossroads of Routes 167 and 168. In the lower picture is a good view of that crossroads. At far left is School No. 7, which was built before the church. In the center is the post office, run for many years by longtime postmaster Albert Krum. When Krum died in 1882, he was succeeded by his wife, Jeanette. (Below, courtesy of Sharon Rolchigo.)

Five

SCHOOLS

FIRST SCHOOLHOUSE. Little Falls' first school was built on this site at the corner of Church and School Streets. In 1814, this stone building was erected on the foundation of the original wooden schoolhouse. After the Free School Bill was passed in 1842, more space was needed, and the Church Street School was built. The old school building was converted into a private residence in 1848 and continues as such today. (Courtesy of LFHS.)

CHURCH STREET SCHOOL. Built in 1848 on the site of the old Octagon Church, the original Church Street School building was replaced with a second school in 1888. Designed by Archimides Russell, it faced Prospect Street and had an entrance on Church Street. With a declining student population, the school closed in 1973. It was sold to Joseph Volo, Inc., in 1976 and razed. (Courtesy of LFHS.)

STUDENTS AT CHURCH STREET SCHOOL, AROUND 1900. Seen here from left to right are students (first row) Lottie Countryman, Olive Wartman, Daisy Dale, Aurelia Shaffer, Lena Van Allen, Nellie Tucker, Zelura Bowers, Lizzie Fallis, Louie Oyston, and Lulu Boyer; (second row) Evelyn Moyer, Agnes Herbert, Josephine Cooper, Marguerite Lower, Grace Thumb, Lena Bailey, Addie Fleming, Eva Van Allen, and Millie DuBois. (Courtesy of LFHS.)

LITTLE FALLS ACADEMY. This private school opened in 1844 on the east side of Eastern Park to offer higher education to local residents. Tuition ranged from $2.50 to $5.50 a semester, depending upon the courses taken. Out-of-town students could rent rooms for an additional $2 a term. In 1868, the academy erected a second building to provide additional rooms for students; it was named Benton Hall in honor of Judge Nathaniel Benton. (Courtesy of LFHS.)

LITTLE FALLS HIGH SCHOOL. Construction began in 1898 on a new public elementary and high school building in front of the old Little Falls Academy. It was completed on August 31, 1900. The grade school was called Benton Hall. A 1929 addition included a gymnasium and auditorium as well as additional classrooms. The building served as the high school until 1970. (Courtesy of LFHS.)

BENTON HALL SCHOOL PLAY, 1932. Shown here from left to right are grade-school thespians (first row) Natlie Brazie, Dorothy Hackett, Dorothy Goldstone, Helen Smeriski, Bill Wing, Bertram Rice, Jack Peterson, and Andrew Little; (second row) Bob Simpson, Barbara Kennedy, Jean Hamilton, Fred Jacox, Muriel Rahm, Roy Watkins, Stella Pratys, Marion Whitcomb, and Harvey Michals. (Courtesy of LFHS.)

LITTLE FALLS BOYS BASKETBALL TEAM, 1925–1926. From left to right, the LFHS squad shown here features (first row) Francis "Humpy" Meade and Morris Goldstein; (second row) Donald Mang, Stanley Rawson, coach Harvey Mills, Oscar Kuhl, and Leon Van Alstyne; (third row) Donald Murray and Charles Clingen. (Courtesy of LFHS.)

LITTLE FALLS HIGH SCHOOL CLASS, 1927. Pictured here from left to right are (first row) Anna Kubica, Sophye Altshuler, Louise Gerssler, Anna Pawelek, Anna Mucica, Robert Woodruff, Helen Abbott, Ada Downs, two unidentified students, and Iva Swartz; (second row) Donald Mang, Helen Finegan, Mary Flynn, Katherine Krueger, Lucille Smith, Doris Wroncy, Sally Teall, Doris Stone, an unidentified student, Agnes Vail, and Charles Hewitt; (third row) an unidentified student, William Klock, Kenneth Stone, Homer Teall, Edward Shumaker, John Babinec, and Russell Derby. (Courtesy of LFHS.)

LITTLE FALLS GIRLS BASKETBALL TEAM, 1925–1926. Boys basketball coach Harvey Mills also coached his squad's female counterparts during the 1925–1926 season. Pictured here from left to right are (first row) Marion Wells and Ruth Bennett; (second row) Doris Stone, Alice Stevenson, coach Mills, Margaret Williams, and Eleanor Eysaman; (third row) Anna Sosin and Emily Sullivan. (Courtesy of LFHS.)

LITTLE FALLS
GIRLS BASKETBALL
TEAM, 1926–1927.
Seen here from
left to right are
basketballers
(first row) Ruth
Bennett and Anna
Halabin; (second
row) Fritz Vickers,
Margaret Williams,
Alice Stevenson,
Liz Scatchard,
and Doris Stone;
(third row) Helen
Finegan, Tubby
Wilcox, Doris
Stahl, and Betty
Wagoner. (Courtesy
of LFHS.)

CLASS OF 1909 50-YEAR REUNION. Shown here from left to right in 1959 are LFHS alumni (first row) Pauline Ferguson, Mrs. Joseph Murphy, Helena Graham, Margaret Clingen, Ethel Rands, Alice Bellinger, Mrs. Lynn Cronkhite, Mrs. Frank Davy, and Marjorie Zoller Smith; (second row) Joseph Murphy, Hazel Mang, Mrs. Griffith Butler, Mrs. Felix Frederiksen, Harold Clingen, Ethel Jenkins, Avery Jenkins, Raymond Bellinger, Lynn Cronkhite, Frank Davy, and Mrs. Harry Dise; (third row) Rev. Philip Mang, Griffith Butler, Felix Frederiksen, James Manning, John Rands, J. Leland Clark, Simon Graham, and Harry Dise. (Courtesy of LFHS.)

LITTLE FALLS BASEBALL TEAM, 1940s. Seen here from left to right are (first row) Johnny Kane, Tommy Kearns, David Rogers, Bill Potter, Ward Hecox, and John Mosny; (second row) Harold Sugar, Don Shepardson, Ray Shepardson, Maurice Vail, Jim Jordan, Mike Lombardi, Gerald Hooks, and Lud Folton. (Courtesy of LFHS.)

LITTLE FALLS BASKETBALL TEAM, 1941. Pictured from left to right are (first row) Steve Remus, John Ostasz, John Bucala, Ed Tedyewski, and Bob Van Slyke; (second row) Mitchell Wojdan, John Brin, unidentified, John Valuck, and unidentified. They had a successful season with a record of 14 wins and 2 losses.

FOOTBALL TEAM, 1943. Shown here from left to right are (first row) Elwood Mueller, John Nemcek, John Valuck, Jack Shaper, Bernard Tracy, Leo Malavasic, Walter Ostasz, Steve Sadlon, Ernie Mueller, and Mike Liscio; (second row) George Helmer, Zigmund Patruska, Bill McEvilly, Mike Spurza, Ed Gaworecki, Dick Schofield, Allen Mueller, Joe Buckley, Kendall Cole, and Marshall Gillette; (third row) Dick Harris, Gerhart Rinke, Dan Herlehy, Charlie Straugh, Adam Gamberdella, Bill Conroy, Vito Blando, Niel Spotten, Armond Chapedeau, Bob Prinsen, Bob Gerbsinski, Milan Mosny, Ed Brown, Gino Pietrapoli, Dick Newhall, Bob Edick, Mike Lamanna, Ted Krohn, Charles Newhall, James Begley, and "Fats" Gabriel. (Courtesy of LFHS.)

JEFFERSON STREET SCHOOL. The school, seen next to the Holy Trinity Church, was built in 1885. Surviving two fires (1908 and 1917) and rebuilt after the second fire, it provided an education for the children on the south side until June 1970. Students then moved to Benton Hall, and the Jefferson Street School was razed in 1971. (Courtesy of LFHS.)

JEFFERSON STREET SCHOOL FIRST GRADE CLASS, 1967–1968. Shown here from left to right are (first row) an unidentified student, Cindy Boepple, Edward Rovetto, Philip Green, and an unidentified student; (second row) Matthew von Wellsheim, Paul Averell, Peter Molinar, Donald Douglas, and Richard Slabe; (third row) Sean ?, Sandy Boepple, Alan Fredericks, Anthony Golosky, and Lorenzo Franci; (fourth row) Robin Critser and Joseph Lawrence; (fifth row) Betsy Casler, Lee Pedersen, Terry Boepple, Alan Rice, and Mary Jo Lonis; (standing) Linda Jasewicz, Paul Restante, Bonnie ?, Sheila Quackenbush, three unidentified students, Dana ?, Natalie ?, and Darlene Diodati. The teacher was Margaret Geisler. (Courtesy of Robin Prinzhorn.)

MONROE STREET SCHOOL. Land for the school was purchased in 1919 on West Monroe Street and was built and ready for its new students in September 1921. It featured six classrooms on each floor and a large athletic field and playground in the back. The school's first principal was Jackson Fenner, and its last was Louis Patrei. (Courtesy of LFHS.)

Monroe Street School Play. With the completion of Benton Hall Academy in 1997, Monroe Street School was the last neighborhood school to close its doors. The Mohawk Valley Christian Academy purchased the school in 1998. Pictured here are cast members of a c. 1929 senior play. From right to left, they are unidentified, Joseph Bennet, Franklin Brownell, Frank Wilcox, Ford Trask, Byron Lally, and Mildred Hurlburt (Whitman). (Courtesy of LFHS.)

St. Mary's Class of 1943. Seen here from left to right are (first row) Richard Eisentraut, Harold Giarrusso, William Wren, Virginia Murphy, Dorothy Kinney, Adele Cannon, Agnes Reardon, Eileen Wren, Rev. William Noonan, Terese Casey, Barbara Perreco, Mary Dorcy, Mary Kearns, William Cutspec, Bernard Hooks, and Maurice Vail; (second row) Mary Grace, Helen Foley, Irene Donnelly, Flavia Vanore, Elizabeth Hartnett, and Verna McCaffery; (third row) Bernard Reardon, Agnes Norwich, Terese Kelly, Mary Potter, and James Keefe; (fourth row) Ray Bacher, James McTiernan, Thomas Vail, and John Murray. (Courtesy of Mary Alice Rieman.)

St. Mary's 1938–1939 Baseball Team. Pictured here from left to right are (first row) Gerald Hooks, Tom Kearns, Gerry Shepardson, Donald Courtney, Roy Griffith, and Bernie Mlinar; (second row) coach Francis Van Allen, Jack Foley, Leo Hooks, Bernie Donnelly, Tom McTiernan, Fr. William Noonan, coach Ray Shepardson, Bill Murphy, Frank Marosek, Peter Moynihan, Bill Shepardson, and manager Bill Courtney. (Courtesy of Peter and Frances Moynihan.)

St. Mary's Class of 1959. Seen here from left to right are (first row) Ann O'Hara, MaryJo Burns, Bill Nash, Fr. Joseph Reger, Msgr. Thomas Scott, Fr. Richard Boyle, Mike Skinner, Janet Waterman, and Janet Mlinar; (second row) Joan Haponski, Carolyn Welch, Catherine Welch, Gaylene Nuborziak, Cornelia Fiesinger, Phyllis Lidden, Cynthia Kane, Monica O'Hara, and Cornelia Demsond; (third row) Tom Finnegan, Dick Hart, Patty Bodosky, JoAnn Clark, Mary Elizabeth Holland, Sarah Falk, Judy Daly, Mike Worden, and Lynne Hebert; (fourth row) Jack Manore, Bill Nash, Jack McCarthy, Denis Sivack, Jim Palmer, Anthony Cooney, and Charlie Fitzgerald Sr. (Courtesy of Charlie and Fran Fitzgerald.)

ST. MARY'S BASEBALL TEAM. Shown here from left to right are (first row) Phil Helmer, manager Brian Guiney, Paul Phillips, Dave Feane, Pat Regan, Mike Mihevic, Tom Hart, and coach Charlie Fitzgerald; (second row) Charles Quatrino, Dave Karpiak, Frank Lawrence, and Tony DeAngeles; (third row) athletic director Rev. Donald Oppels, Jim Rieman, and manager Rich Mlinar. (Courtesy of Charlie and Fran Fitzgerald.)

NEW LITTLE FALLS HIGH SCHOOL. The Little Falls Junior-Senior High School, pictured at far right, was opened on Top Notch Road in 1970. Built using an innovative design concept of open classrooms, the school had a capacity for 1,000 students, grades 7–12. The large auditorium featured a suspended ceiling to provide better acoustics. The new gymnasium, with a bleacher capacity of 1,000, featured Uni-Turf covering one section. (Courtesy of *The Times*.)

HIGH SCHOOL FIRE. On January 10, 1976, a fire broke out in the school, destroying two-thirds of the building. The roof over the central portion of the building collapsed, leaving only the auditorium and some adjacent classrooms at the east end and the gymnasium at the west end. The students attended classes at Benton Hall while the school was being rebuilt. (Courtesy of *The Times*.)

BENTON HALL GRADE SCHOOL. By the 1990s, the school was badly in need of updating. It was decided to do a major renovation of the three existing buildings rather than demolition. Working with the New York State Historic Preservation Office, architects were able to accurately reproduce the structure, still known as Benton Hall Academy, while providing thoroughly modern educational facilities for the students of Little Falls. (Courtesy of Benton Hall Academy.)

INTERIOR. Opened in 1997, the completely renovated Benton Hall Academy boasts the Leon Dussault Auditorium, Wilbur Crisp Gymnasium, and Dr. Bernard Burke Library. The auditorium's original seating was removed and returned to its manufacturer in Canada for restoration before being reinstalled. The school project was awarded a national architectural citation by the American Association of School Administrators, American Institute of Architects, and Council of Educational Facility Planners. (Courtesy of Benton Hall Academy.)

LITTLE FALLS SYMPHONY ORCHESTRA. The symphony began in 1928, when violin pupils of Leon Dussault and piano pupils of Edith Ward gave a joint recital. Some professional musicians offered to join the group to form an orchestra, and they went on to play for 43 years. Musical director Dussault's contributions to music were honored by naming the high school auditorium after him. The orchestra discontinued in 1971. (Courtesy of Frances and Peter Moynihan.)

Six

BUSINESS AND INDUSTRY

HINCHMAN HOUSE. This hotel was first built in 1840 at 557 East Main Street by Charles Hinchman, who left it to his wife and daughters upon his death in 1855. A fire destroyed the hotel in 1866, and the family rebuilt it (as seen here), but it burned again in 1877. George Shall then purchased the Hinchman property and converted two stores into a hotel, which he ran until 1891, when he leased it to Lasher and Weatherwax. They changed the name to Hotel Rockton. Today the former hotel location is the site of Shopper's Square. (Courtesy of LFHS.)

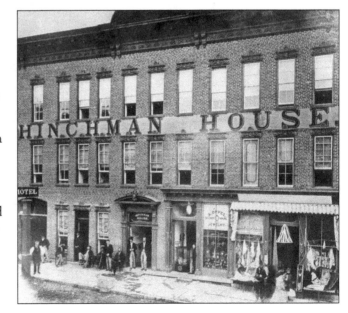

CRONKHITE OPERA HOUSE.
The opera house was opened by
William Cronkhite (1853–1901)
in 1871 on the corner of South
Ann and Main Streets. In 1882,
it was illuminated by electricity,
a major improvement over gas
lighting. In 1918, the building,
which also housed the Little Falls
National Bank, suffered a major
fire. This c. 1916 photograph
shows Leland Cassidy's grocery
store on the first floor and Dr.
Henry Terry's dentist office on the
second floor. (Courtesy of LFHS.)

LITTLE FALLS NATIONAL BANK. Organized in December 1878, LFNB started business in the
Cronkhite Opera House block. On November 11, 1918, fire damaged the building, and the bank
moved to the old Herkimer County Bank site on South Ann Street. A new building was constructed
and opened on June 19, 1921. The bank changed hands when it became Oneida National (1979),
Norstar (1985), Fleet (1997), and Bank of America (2004). (Courtesy of LFHS.)

EVENING TIMES. This newspaper started production on May 10, 1886, under its first editor, John Devlin. The offices and presses were first located on Mary Street and later moved to 595 East Main Street. By 1897, the paper was located on the corner of John and Second Streets. That building is pictured here with the newspaper's staff. *The Times* continued to keep its offices there until 2009. In 1940, John McGurie became the paper's publisher. Ralph Weir served as editor for many years until his retirement in 1992. (Courtesy of *The Times*.)

GEORGE ARROW
BARBERSHOP. In this 1922 photograph, Frank Donadio (1885–1976) is seen in the barbershop of his uncle George Arrow (1859–1946) at 403 South Ann Street. George was born in Italy with the surname of Laranga, arriving in the United States in 1882. He came to Little Falls in 1903. Frank was also born in Italy and later became a mason and worked for several area contractors. (Courtesy of Phyllis Shelton.)

ELLIS GROCERY STORE. Edward Ellis (1864-1947) opened this grocery around 1903 at 109 West John Street. Pictured from left to right are Thomas Kenneally (clerk), Claude Ellis (son), Edward Ellis, Ed Ellis (son), and Ed Buckley (clerk). Ellis sold the business to Kenneally, who operated it until around 1916, when he moved his store up the street. Ellis moved to Herkimer, where he operated a grocery at 246 North Main Street. (Courtesy of LFHS)

A&P STORE. In this c. 1917 photograph, William Parker Barry stands proudly in front of the Great Atlantic and Pacific Tea Company store he manages at 8 North Ann Street. A&P was the first grocery chain to reach coach to coast. It had several locations in Little Falls over the years, but the best-remembered one operated at 633 East Main Street from the 1940s up to 1964, when it was razed for construction of Shopper's Square. (Courtesy of Barry Dawson.)

TRUMAN COLE MERCANTILE COMPANY. Truman Cole (1862–1945) started a farm hardware store around 1913 that specialized in feed and flour and the sale of agricultural implements, wagons, harnesses, saddlery, auto supplies, and Ford automobiles. His store was located at 532–534 Albany Street. In 1918, the store was incorporated as the Truman Cole Mercantile Company. Cole served as alderman for the city and was a director of the YMCA for many years. He also helped organize the United Dairymen's Association, a cooperative group for marketing fluid milk in New York, and served as its first president. The picture above shows the storefront with Truman Cole (left) and his son Carlton standing outside. The picture below shows the interior of the store with Truman standing behind the counter. (Courtesy of Kendall Cole.)

SCARANO BAKERY. Immigrants from Modillion, Italy, brothers Rocco and Luciano Scarano founded a bakery at 17 Flint Avenue in 1913. The business flourished with specially made breads, turning out close to 1,000 loaves per day at its peak. They expanded the store to include gasoline, groceries, and a meat market and made deliveries throughout the city and surrounding area. Throughout the war years and the Depression, the Scaranos extended credit to their customers in need; these were graciously forgiven after the business closed in 1968. The photograph above shows Rocco and Luciano Scarano in their store. The bakery was in the back, and the meat case stands behind the tins of olive oil. (Courtesy of Rocco Scarano.)

HALL'S TAXI AND SERVICE STATION. Orval Hall (1906–1979) opened up a taxi stand and convenience store (below) on the corner of Ann and Church Streets in the 1930s. By the 1940s, he was able to expand his business to two taxi stands, opening one on the corner of East Main and Second Streets across from Lurie's (above). Orville maintained a parking lot next to his station, but people would often leave their cars there for nothing because he didn't have the manpower to staff it. He expanded further to a Dodge and Plymouth car dealership on the corner of Garden and Second Streets. In 1964, he combined his businesses at the Main Street location. An Atlantic service station occupied the North Ann Street site. In the 1980s, it became the Convenient Food Mart. In 1995, it became Xtra-Mart. (Below, courtesy of LFHS.)

GULF BRIDGE GARAGE. The garage in this 1936 photograph, located at the corner of East Main and Ward Streets (806 East Main), was operated by Jay Brown. He started the business in the early 1920s as an auto accessories store and expanded to a full-service garage. Jay and his family lived upstairs. The last owner of the building was Fred Giarrusso, who operated it as Fred's Garage. It closed in the mid-1940s. (Courtesy of Patricia Carey.)

RESTANTE'S DAIRY. Paul Restante started his career working for Little Falls Dairy. By 1942, he purchased Albrecht's Dairy Processing plant and started processing milk with sons Paul Jr. and John. In 1952, Restante's Dairy Bar opened on 67 Flint Avenue featuring milk, cream, buttermilk, and homemade ice cream. Restante's Dairy continued to deliver milk to Little Falls residents until the death of Paul Sr. in 1973. (Courtesy of Dolores Restante.)

PAPALEO'S. A popular gathering place in the 1960s and 1970s, Papaleo's has the unique feature of being in a renovated train station on South Ann Street. Anthony Papaleo (1913–1990) operated the business for 25 years and was well known for his pizza and other Italian specialties. In later years, it became the Riviera Restorante and then Ruggerio's. In 1994, Piccolo Café opened here.

EAST MAIN STREET BUSINESSES. East Main Street is pictured at the corner of Ann Street before the buildings on the right were demolished for urban renewal in the 1970s. Main Street at that time was Route 5 and was a two-way street. Some of the businesses on the right were the mansard-roofed Lurie's (which had Falls Bowling upstairs), Diana's Restaurant, Yourdon's, Ackerman's, Clemens Drug Store, and City Cigar Store.

LOBLAW'S. A Canadian grocery chain that came to the United States in 1928, Loblaw's opened a location at 597 East Main Street in the 1940s. It did business there until 1964, when the store was taken down for the first phase of urban renewal for Shopper's Square. Pictured from left to right are Bernie Crimmins, Stella ?, Agnes Ehlinger, Mary Alice Rieman, Jack Roche, Dick Primmar, Bob Peterson, unidentified, Gladys Stahl, and unidentified. (Courtesy of LFHS.)

BOBER'S MARKET. John Bober (1894–1964) opened up a meat market at 28 West John Street in the 1930s with his wife, Mary (Kobylarz). John's son Boleshaw took part in the business, and in 1961, grandson Joseph Lasowski took it over. He expanded the store to a full line of groceries and beverages and specialized in custom-cut meats. The market closed when the building was taken down during urban renewal in 1970. (Courtesy of LFHS.)

RIALTO THEATRE. A popular spot on North Ann Street for many years, the Rialto Theatre is a truly missed Little Falls landmark. Built by James Hallinan, it first opened its doors in 1923 as the Gateway Theatre. The Schine Theatre Corporation purchased it in 1925 and hung the large electric sign on the outside. In addition to films, vaudeville acts entertained audiences at the Rialto. Shown here is the line for a 1945 Saturday matinee. The theater's popular serials were shown weekly, with each episode's ending leaving audiences on the edges of their seats. The Rialto changed ownership over the years and was finally closed on Memorial Day, 1972. It deteriorated after closing and had to be razed in 1997. (Below, courtesy of *The Times*.)

LITTLE FALLS HARDWARE. This popular hardware store was owned by Edwin Metott (1914–1995) and his wife, Amelia (1915–1974). Originally located at 307 South Second Street in the 1950s, the store moved to 517 East Main Street in 1965 with a grand opening, shown here. By the early 1970s, the store had moved to Route 5S between Little Falls and Herkimer. Today the store, run by Jim Metott, is located at 528 East Main Street in Little Falls. (Courtesy of Little Falls Hardware.)

ROCKTON KNITTING MILL. Seated from left to right in the sleigh are Walter Ward Whitman (1845–1918) and his brother Rodney Whitman (1835–1918). The sleigh sits in front of the office of Rockton Mills, formed in 1891 and located on Mohawk Street. The office was torn down for the construction of the Barge Canal, and the mills were taken down when the canal was widened in 1938. (Courtesy of LFHS.)

Little Falls Knitting Company. This photograph shows company employees gathered by the factory along the Mohawk River on Elizabeth Street. The facility was originally built by Charles Bailey (1830–1924) and Jeremiah Mitchell (1831–1879) for the manufacture of shoddy, but in 1872, they formed a knitting company with businessmen Titus Sheard and J. J. Gilbert. Bailey remained president until he moved to Fort Plain in 1899. Thereafter, the building became part of the Gilbert Knitting Company. (Courtesy of LFHS.)

H. P. Snyder Manufacturing. This picture shows the end of this renowned company, which had manufactured bicycles for nearly 80 years when it was taken down in 1977. In 1890, Homer P. Snyder and Michael Fisher erected a factory to make knitting machines, but by 1895, it had been refitted to make bicycles. The following year, Snyder became sole owner of the company, and it became the largest producer and distributor of bicycles in the world. (Courtesy of LFHS.)

H. P. Snyder Foremen, 1930s. Shown here are the foremen of the company at the Yahnundasis Club in New Hartford. From left to right, they are (first row) Ed Haug, Lorenzo Fox, Homer Teall, E. S. Van Valkenburg, Bill Snyder, Owen Sperbeck, and Ed Haggerty; (second row) Lyle Jones, Mr. Reinhardt, Harry Carden, Harry Baker, Charles Spraker, Gus Clifford, John Sullivan, Bill Elias, and Bill Campbell. (Courtesy of LFHS.)

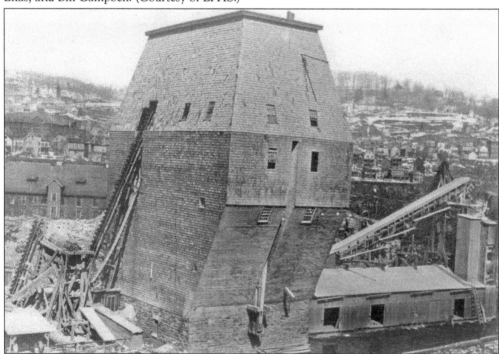

Gilbert's Grain Elevator. Joshua Gilbert Sr. (1821–1881) came to Little Falls in 1854 from Utica to build a factory to manufacture cornstarch on Seeley Island. He built this grain elevator to store and convey the grain from the Erie Canal to the factory. In 1888, Gilbert's son converted the starch works into the Asteronga Knitting Mill. The grain elevator stood until 1912, when it was demolished for the Barge Canal. (Courtesy of LFHS.)

GILBERT KNITTING MILL. The Little Falls Knitting Company was the predecessor of the Gilbert Knitting Mill, shown here, at 151 Elizabeth Street. Joshua Gilbert Jr. (1861–1925) acquired the mill in 1899 and reorganized it a year later as the Gilbert Knitting Company. That year, a 100-foot-by-100-foot, four-story addition was added to the mill. The company was sold in 1963. Several other businesses have since occupied the building.

LITTLE FALLS FELT SHOE COMPANY. Located at Sixth and West John Streets, this company was organized in 1905 by brothers Irving Stacey (1864–1938) and Frank Stacey, along with Frank Engel, formerly president of Dolgeville Felt Shoe Company. Manufacturers of felt shoes and slippers, by 1938, the company was producing over 3 million pairs annually. The company closed its Little Falls factory in 1962 to consolidate its operations in St. Johnsville. (Courtesy of Nancy Cioch.)

ZOLLER PACKING HOUSE. The Zoller Packing House, at 561–571 Mill Street, was built in 1881 by Jacob Zoller (1833–1907). The company manufactured and distributed cheese, beef and pork products, butter, and eggs. It was also a wholesale grocer. It was one of the first in the area to install a cold storage system. Notice the trolley tracks and the Wonder Bread billboard in the foreground with its slogan, "It's Slo-baked." (Courtesy of LFHS.)

BEGINNINGS OF D. H. BURRELL AND COMPANY. Rodney Whitman partnered with David H. Burrell to purchase the George Ashley hardware store on Main Street in 1868. They immediately began to add dairy supplies to their stock, and the firm grew. In 1880, they sold the hardware business and purchased the Presbyterian church on the corner of Albany and Ann Streets, where they built a factory complex to manufacture and sell dairy supplies. (Courtesy of LFHS.)

EXPANSION OF FACTORY.
In 1885, Burrell and his brother Edward became the factory's sole owners, and the firm name changed to D. H. Burrell and Company. The company eventually expanded to include the entire block along Albany Street from Ann Street to Second Street. It developed and sold everything required in the milk business: cheese boxes, cheese presses, the first centrifugal cream separator, pasteurizing equipment, and milking machines. (Courtesy of LFHS.)

CONTINUING DEVELOPMENT IN THE DAIRY INDUSTRY. The Burrell Company was instrumental in developing milk pasteurizing systems and introduced a horse-drawn tank truck to ship bulk milk into city milk plants. It developed a power-operated machine called the BLK Milker in 1905. The company introduced stainless steel as a substitute for tinned copper in the manufacture of dairy and food equipment. (Courtesy of LFHS.)

MERGER. In 1928, D. H. Burrell and Company joined with the two other major firms (the J. G. Cherry Company of Cedar Rapids, Iowa, and Milwaukee Dairy Supply of Milwaukee, Wisconsin) and four distributor companies to form the Cherry-Burrell Corporation. Loomis Burrell was its first chairman. In 1947, it built this new factory on East Mill Street; by 1958, the old Albany Street buildings were closed. (Courtesy of LFHS.)

CHERRY-BURRELL EMPLOYEES. Pictured here are a number of company employees in 1947. From left to right, they are (first row) Charles Fogarty and unidentified; (second row) Ron Senft, Staring Shunk, Ron Williams, Burdette Balderston, Clarence Kohn, Walter Wiesinski, and Bill Sivack; (third row) Joe Yacobucci, Jim Evans, Al Graudons, Bob Ruppert, Luke Zambri, Peter Moynihan, and Vince Perrino. (Courtesy of Frances and Peter Moynihan.)

FELDMEIER EQUIPMENT. In 1998, Feldmeier Equipment, Inc., purchased Cherry-Burrell's Little Falls plant. Founder Robert Feldmeier was a sales engineer for Cherry-Burrell after World War II before starting his company. From 1894 to 1935, his father, Harvey Feldmeier, was chief engineer for the D. H. Burrell Company and then for Cherry-Burrell. Today Feldmeier Equipment manufactures 1,200–1,400 stainless steel vessels annually for the dairy, food, pharmaceutical, and beverage industries. Pictured is Feldmeier employee Randy Johnson. (Courtesy of Feldmeier Equipment.)

BURRELL BUILDING. David H. Burrell commissioned this building to be built on the corner of North Ann and East Main Streets for the Herkimer County Trust Company (HCT), opened on April 30, 1917. Burrell, a bank chairman, was the first depositor. HCT's new headquarters opened across the street on March 29, 1976. They merged with Savings Bank of Utica (SBU) in 2002 and later were purchased by Partners Trust (2004) and Manufacturers and Traders (M&T) Bank (2007).

CHRISTIAN HANSEN'S LABORATORY. In the early 1870s, Danish pharmaceutical chemist Christian Hansen came up with a breakthrough method of making a uniform rennet extract that allowed uniform results in cheese production. He started manufacturing the product in 1874; in 1878, he sent Johan Frederiksen to the United States as his American agent. In 1881, Frederiksen moved the business to Little Falls, which was the center of the cheese business on the eastern seaboard. The company purchased Lock Island, and work began in 1890 on a new factory as well as a retaining wall around the island. In 1892, Little Falls provided an old iron railroad bridge obtained from the Delaware and Hudson Railroad Company to connect Lock Street to Hansen Island. Over the years, Hansen's company introduced cheese rennet tables and Junket rennet tables for household use. (Courtesy of LFHS.)

COMPANY EXPANSION. The company quickly grew, and additions were made to the factory complex. By 1937, it was necessary to construct a more modern addition of glass brick, completely air-conditioned, for sanitary food production purposes. Johannes Hansen succeeded his father as president in 1916. Chief chemist Karl Monrad took over the posts of general manager and treasurer when Frederiksen retired in 1924, and he later became the company's executive vice president. The laboratory developed new products such as Junket Freezing Mix (for ice cream) and Junket Quick Fudge and Frosting Mix. A new dairy-preparations factory was built in Milwaukee, and a factory was set up in Toronto, Canada. In 1951, a concrete-block warehouse was constructed on Route 5 west of Little Falls. Salada-Shirriff-Horsey acquired the Junket Brand Foods Division of Christian Hansen's Laboratory in 1958. (Courtesy of LFHS.)

BURROWS PAPER CORPORATION. Charles Burrows (1870–1958) came to Little Falls in 1913 as the principal stockholder in the newly formed Mohawk Valley Paper Company on West Main Street (above), specializing in high-grade tissues. In 1920, Burrows partnered with his brother Andrew (1883–1949) to take over the Little Falls Paper Company's plant on East Mill Street, and they incorporated under the name Burrows Paper Corporation (left). The primary products were gift-wrap tissue paper, pattern tissue paper for the sewing industry, and a line of sanitary tissue products known as Burline Tissues. (Courtesy of Burrows Paper Corporation.)

COMPANY EXPANDS. From 1952 through 1986, Ralph Burrows, son of Andrew, expanded the company's operations. He purchased the Mohawk Valley Paper Company (1952); a mill in Lyonsdale, New York (1966); and a mill in Pickens, Mississippi (1967). The product line expanded to include one-time carbonizing tissue as well as other specialty tissue grades. Ralph's son, Bill Burrows, succeeded to the presidency in 1976. The company purchased Midwest Packaging Materials Company of Fort Madison, Iowa, in 1986, expanding the product line to include fast-food packaging papers. Seven years later, it purchased Corroc International of Franklin, Ohio, to further expand the product line to include micro-flute corrugated clamshell boxes for food packaging. The company still continues to manufacture specialty tissue papers at two mills in Little Falls—one on West Main Street (above) and another on East Mill Street (below). (Courtesy of LFHS.)

ALLEGRO SHOE COMPANY. In 1900, Robert MacKinnon constructed this building on the corner of South Ann and West Mill Streets. It served as a knitting mill employing over 1,000 workers. From 1910 to 1928, the factory was owned by the Phoenix Underwear Company. In 1934, the Little Falls Industrial Committee brought in Melrose Slipper Company to operate the site, which it did until 1949. After this, the Cosmos Shoe Company of New York formed the Allegro Shoe Corporation and occupied the building. A leading U.S. shoe producer, in 1958, Allegro produced 15,000 pairs of shoes a day and over 6.3 million pairs for the year. Allegro moved its operation in 1974, leaving the building vacant. In 1987, the Herkimer County Industrial Development Agency demolished the structure (left) to create room for parking and business expansion. (Above, courtesy of LFHS; left, courtesy of *The Times*.)

ANDREW LITTLE AND SONS. In 1881, Andrew Little (1837–1935) formed a partnership with Charles Newell to operate a planing mill on West Mill Street. Andrew became the sole proprietor in 1892, manufacturing sashes, doors, blinds, and all parts of house woodwork. The company also engaged in logging. The above picture shows Little's employees in 1905. Andrew's son Gordon (1887–1977) later took over the business. In 1938, the company built an office and storage building across the street. Andrew Little and Sons was the last of many mills to use the Mill Street raceway for waterpower; it finally converted to electric in 1960. The business continued as a family-operated enterprise until the 1980s. In the mid-1990s, Little Falls Construction took over the site. (Courtesy of LFHS.)

LITTLE FALLS HOSPITAL. The hospital began in 1893 when a group of 17 women, headed by Mrs. E. B. Waite, rented and renovated this house on 14 North Ann Street as a hospital. Incorporated the following year, Little Falls Hospital occupied this four-bed facility until 1896, when it moved to larger accommodations at 610 East Monroe Street. The first patient admitted at Ann Street was suffering from typhoid fever. (Courtesy of LFHS.)

HOSPITAL MOVES TO BURWELL STREET. By 1905, a new building was constructed at the corner of Burwell and Whited Streets. Originally a two-story, gable-roofed building, in 1908, the structure was renovated to provide a full third story for hospital use. During the influenza epidemic of 1918, the hospital set up visiting nurse services that operated around the clock for three weeks.

New Hospital. Further additions were made to the hospital in 1924 and 1938, more than doubling its size. In 1962, this five-story steel west wing was added, expanding the hospital's capacity to 110 beds. In 1974, the original hospital building was demolished and replaced by a new east wing. In 2009, a new handicapped-accessible entrance was constructed.

Donations of Equipment. Many groups and individuals donated funds and equipment to the Little Falls Hospital over the years. This orthopedic table was donated by Little Falls American Legion Post No. 31. From left to right are Dr. J. J. McEvilley, Dr. Fred Sabin, Arthur McLaughlin, Mae Simpson (president of the board of trustees), Hazel Noyes, RN, Dr. Morris Newton, Cordelia King (hospital superintendent), and Judge Bernard Malone. (Courtesy of LFHS.)

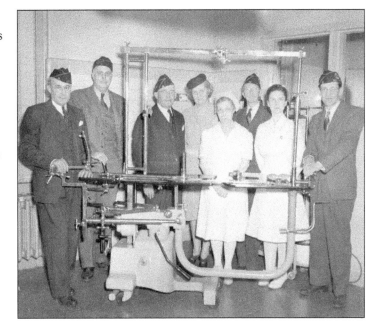

RADIO STATION. In 1952, Arthur Feldman (1915–2006) and his brother Robert (1919–2008) built a broadcasting tower behind the family's furniture and appliance store at the corner of Albany and Second Streets. On June 22 of that year, radio station WLFH began broadcasting to area residents—the first full-time radio station in Herkimer County. Although the station changed ownership several times, it continued to broadcast news and music to area residents for generations. Under Roser Communications, WOW-FM 105.5 was added in 1993. Today only the transmitter is still in Little Falls under the call letters WIXT (1230 AM). Some well-known WLFH radio personalities are seen in the picture above. From left to right, they are Gary Van Veghten (station manager from 1982 to 1990), disc jockey Chris Miller (1980–1986), and disc jockey and program director Bill Keeler (1982–1989). (Above, courtesy of Gary Van Veghten; left, courtesy of LFHS.)

Seven

TRANSPORTATION

WESTERN INLAND LOCK NAVIGATION COMPANY (WILNC). The first canal built at Little Falls was constructed by the Western Inland Lock Navigation Company (1792–1821). It was not a canal in the usual sense; it only provided short sections of waterway that bypassed the various falls and rapids in the Mohawk River. This photograph shows a bridge over part of the canal at East Mill Street (Courtesy of LFHS.)

ERIE CANAL. The Erie Canal officially opened on October 26, 1825. Previous to the Erie Canal enlargement in 1841, Seeley Island, pictured here, was in the center of the Mohawk River. Dykes were built at each end, turning the Mohawk into the northern channel and canal into the southern channel. Pictured is Gilbert's grain elevator, which was removed when the Barge Canal was built. (Courtesy of LFHS.)

BARGE CANAL LOCK 17. By the early 1900s, the Erie Canal could not accommodate the much larger vessels of the day and was rapidly becoming obsolete. To remedy the problem, the state began construction of a huge barge canal. The newly constructed Lock 17, with its unique overhead gate, replaced the old system of four locks. At the time of its construction, it was the highest single lift of any lock in the world. (Courtesy of LFHS.)

Moss Island. Standing on a rock ledge on Moss Island are (left to right) Edward Cooney, city historian, Dr. Albert Corey, state historian, and Donald Hurley discussing plans for a canal museum there in 1959. The island is home to unique geological formations known as "pot holes" that were formed by the swirling action of water during the receding of glaciers of the last Ice Age. The island was recognized by the National Park Service in 1976 as a national natural landmark.

Little Falls Aqueduct. An aqueduct over the Mohawk River was constructed in 1823 to serve as a feeder to the Erie Canal on the river's south side, ferrying small cargo ships into a docking basin. It was used for close to 50 years before it was drained in 1871. Parts of the aqueduct were dismantled when businesses along the river needed to expand. The last remnant of the aqueduct fell into the river on November 30, 1993. (Courtesy of LFHS.)

SOUTH ANN STREET BRIDGE. This bridge is located at the site of one of the earliest crossings to the south side of the Mohawk. A stone bridge was erected in 1832 when the previous bridge collapsed. A new iron bridge was built in 1893. In 1933, the bridge's steelwork had to be torn out and replaced. In 2010, the aging bridge again faced repairs and was limited to one-lane traffic. (Courtesy of LFHS.)

SOUTH WILLIAM STREET BRIDGE. This iron bridge was constructed in 1886 and is still standing, but it is no longer open to traffic. It led from East Mill Street over the Mohawk River to Seeley Street. It was closed to traffic around 1958. In the background is the Barnet Leather Company, started in 1877 by brothers Jonas Barnet (1849–1905) and Morris Barnet (1856–1921). The tannery and equipment were auctioned for sale in 1933.

LIFT BRIDGE. From 1913 to 1964, the Lift Bridge was a unique fixture on the south side in Little Falls. Constructed to accommodate the new Barge Canal, it connected Mohawk Street to East Jefferson Street and Flint Avenue, and its center span could be elevated to permit passage of Barge Canal boats. After the new Route 167 arterial bridge opened in the summer of 1964, the Lift Bridge was taken down. (Courtesy of LFHS.)

EMERGENCY BRIDGE. This bridge, constructed in 1913, connected East Jefferson Street with South Ann Street. The state barricaded the bridge to car traffic in 1979. When it was taken down in August 1980, the bridge was cut from its approach, lifted by two cranes, and loaded onto a barge. The water level in the canal had to be lowered for it to pass beneath the arterial bridge. (Courtesy of LFHS.)

HANSEN'S BRIDGE. The Hansen Island Double Bridge connected Christian Hansen's laboratory with Southern Avenue over the Barge Canal. In 1909, the state acquired a former railroad bridge and sent it up on a barge to where it was put in place, as seen here. It was removed in 1964. On the other side of the island was a bridge connecting the island to West Main Street via Lock Street. In 1938 and 1939, a smaller, PWA-funded bridge was built to replace this one. (Courtesy of LFHS.)

SUSPENSION BRIDGE. In the early 1800s, travelers would cross the Mohawk River at Finck's Basin aboard a ferry run by Andrew Finck. A bridge was built in 1828. Since that time, several bridges at the site have been destroyed by floods and ice jams. A suspension bridge, shown here, was finally built in 1869 and 1870. The buildings at the left in this photograph belong to the Riverside Hotel, previously known as Finck's Tavern.

FIRE STRIKES BRIDGE. The suspension bridge stood for nearly half a century until it was destroyed by fire in 1917. The state built an iron bridge over the canalized river and held opening ceremonies on October 4, 1918, with the Slovenian Band furnishing music for the occasion. (Courtesy of Lil Gaherty.)

NEW FINCK'S BASIN BRIDGE. The bridge not only provided a connecting route for residents of Danube and the vicinity to Little Falls, but it would also become a main route to the New York State Thruway. When the new Theodore Wind Connector Bridge opened in 1982, redirecting the heavy traffic, the bridge was closed. For some time it had been one-way with traffic lights at both ends. It was torn down in 1983. (Courtesy of LFHS.)

NEW YORK STATE THRUWAY CONNECTOR BRIDGE. Climaxing a battle over unique geological formations on Moss Island, the state department of transportation and the city agreed on an alternate route for the bridge that would not cross over the island. Construction began just east of Lock 17 in 1979. The bridge was a final phase of an extensive arterial system in Little Falls and would allow easier access between the city and the New York State Thruway interchange. (Courtesy of LFHS.)

BRIDGE NAMED FOR THEODORE WIND. Named in honor of the former Little Falls mayor for his efforts to get a New York State Thruway exit built to Little Falls, the Theodore Wind Connector Bridge opened for traffic with a ribbon ceremony on July 2, 1982. The bridge stretches from Route 5 across the railroad tracks, River Road, and the Barge Canal/Mohawk River.

FLINT AVENUE TO ROUTE 5S. This pastoral view of the Mohawk Valley shows Route 5S in the foreground and Flint Avenue at right. Before the Route 167 arterial was opened in 1964, Flint Avenue was the entrance to the city from south of the river. The city can be seen in the upper center. The West Shore railroad traces along the river's southern bank. (Courtesy of LFHS.)

OVERHEAD CROSSING. Albany Street was extended to an overhead crossing as part of the New York Central's project to eliminate dangerous grade crossings in 1938. The crossing came to a "T" with two routes down to the south side, as seen in this aerial picture. This picture also shows the South Ann Street Bridge in the center and the Emergency Bridge nearby. (Courtesy of LFHS.)

RIVER ROAD WAS MAIN ROUTE. River Road was the main route (Route 5) from Little Falls heading east. Shown is the original Main Street as it entered River Road with the Little Falls–Dolgeville Railroad bridge overhead. The short, deep Gulf Hill, the narrow, curving road, and potholes caused accident hazards, but the major problem was the low railroad bridges that caught the tops of large trucks passing underneath. (Courtesy of LFHS.)

NEW ROUTE 5. The state decided to build a new highway connecting Route 5 through Little Falls to alleviate the River Road traffic problems. Construction began in 1937. Callanan Road Improvement Company was awarded the project, and they would face the great obstacle of blasting through the tremendous rock foundations of the Burnt Rocks just outside the city. Pictured is the area before construction showing Petrie Street. (Courtesy of Lil Gaherty.)

GORGE VIEW HIGHWAY. The new highway, locally known as the "Gorge View," would four traffic lanes wide, the first of its kind in Herkimer County. The deepest cut ever made for a highway in New York State at that time was blasted through the hardest rock, known as syenite-trap rock, for the highway. It was finally completed and officially opened to the public on September 20, 1938. Hundreds of cars and trucks participated in a huge motorcade for a trip of inspection after a ceremony and ribbon cutting were held by state and city officials. The highway coincided with the opening of the overhead crossing of the New York Central railroad tracks and pedestrian subway at Ann Street as part of a project aimed at eliminating railroad crossings in the city. (Courtesy of Lil Gaherty.)

TROLLEY SERVICE. The first electric trolley entered Little Falls on April 29, 1903, as seen above. A large interurban car carried dignitaries on the first day, but subsequent service was provided by smaller cars, as the larger cars were deemed too heavy to safely cross the canal and river bridges. On that first day, crowds lined Main Street, church bells rang, and cannons fired a salute as the car passed Eastern Park. The Utica and Mohawk Valley Electric Railroad stretched 37 miles from Little Falls to Rome, providing service every half hour. The line prospered until the popularity of the automobile forced its closing in 1933. The lower picture shows the trolley tracks on East John Street by St. Mary's Church on the day of Rev. Thomas Farrell's funeral in September 1910. (Courtesy of LFHS.)

NEW YORK CENTRAL RAILROAD. In 1853, the New York Central Railroad was formed by Wall Street entrepreneurs through the consolidation of 12 lines, including the Utica and Schenectady, which ran through Herkimer County. Work began in 1873 on a second set of double tracks between Albany and Buffalo, making it the first four-tracked railroad in the world. The passenger depot was located on the north side of the tracks until 1894–1895, when it was moved between Ann and Second Streets to replace the freight station located there. The freight station was rebuilt between Fifth and Sixth Streets. By the time New York Central merged with the Pennsylvania Railroad to form Penn Central in 1968, local passenger service in Little Falls had stopped. In 1971, Amtrak absorbed passenger operations. In 1976, Conrail was formed to handle freight. (Above, courtesy of LFHS; below, courtesy of Nancy Cioch.)

LITTLE FALLS–DOLGEVILLE RAILROAD. Construction began in 1891 with initial chief investors Judge Hardin, Schuyler Ingham, and Alfred Dolge. The line, seen at far right, opened December 14, 1892, and connected with the New York Central through an interchange at Little Falls. On April 10, 1898, the railroad passed into receivership. The New York Central took over operations in 1913. Passenger service ended in 1933; freight service ceased on July 14, 1964. (Courtesy of LFHS.)

WEST SHORE RAILROAD. In 1880, Edward Winslow of New York formed the New York, West Shore, and Buffalo Railway. Construction began in 1881. It officially opened its line between Albany and Syracuse on October 3, 1883, carrying freight and passengers. The line had been in operation between New York and Albany since July. Rugene Walrath was the first to purchase a ticket to New York at the Little Falls station. (Courtesy of Nancy Cioch.)

WEST SHORE ROUTE. The difficult winter of 1883–1884 reduced freight revenues, and a rate war between the Central and West Shore ensued. On June 9, 1884, the West Shore was declared bankrupt. On December 5, 1885, it was sold to J. Pierpont Morgan, Chauncey Depew, and Ashbel Green as joint tenants. They formed the West Shore Railroad Company and leased it to the New York Central. (Courtesy of LFHS.)

WEST SHORE DEPOT. A temporary depot was set up for the railway's opening while the new one was being built. Passenger travel ended after World War II but was sometimes resurrected whenever the Central's main line was tied up. Freight ran on the West Shore until the early 1960s. The line ceased operation in 1966. The City of Little Falls built a bicycle trail along the roadbed in 1988. (Courtesy of LFHS.)

Visit us at
arcadiapublishing.com